ROUTLEDGE LIBRARY EDITIONS: PHONETICS AND PHONOLOGY

Volume 18

STUDIES IN TIER STRUCTURE

STUDIES IN TIER STRUCTURE

R. ARMIN MESTER

LONDON AND NEW YORK

First published in 1988 by Garland Publishing, Inc.

This edition first published in 2019
by Routledge
2 Park Square, Milton Park, Abingdon, Oxon OX14 4RN

and by Routledge
711 Third Avenue, New York, NY 10017

Routledge is an imprint of the Taylor & Francis Group, an informa business

© 1988 R. Armin Mester

All rights reserved. No part of this book may be reprinted or reproduced or utilised in any form or by any electronic, mechanical, or other means, now known or hereafter invented, including photocopying and recording, or in any information storage or retrieval system, without permission in writing from the publishers.

Trademark notice: Product or corporate names may be trademarks or registered trademarks, and are used only for identification and explanation without intent to infringe.

British Library Cataloguing in Publication Data
A catalogue record for this book is available from the British Library

ISBN: 978-1-138-60364-6 (Set)
ISBN: 978-0-429-43708-3 (Set) (ebk)
ISBN: 978-1-138-60426-1 (Volume 18) (hbk)
ISBN: 978-1-138-60428-5 (Volume 18) (pbk)
ISBN: 978-0-429-46857-5 (Volume 18) (ebk)

Publisher's Note
The publisher has gone to great lengths to ensure the quality of this reprint but points out that some imperfections in the original copies may be apparent.

Disclaimer
The publisher has made every effort to trace copyright holders and would welcome correspondence from those they have been unable to trace.

Studies in Tier Structure

R. Armin Mester

Garland Publishing, Inc. ■ New York & London
1988

Copyright © 1988 R. Armin Mester
All Rights Reserved

Library of Congress Cataloging-in-Publication Data

Mester, Ralf-Armin.
  Studies in tier structure / R. Armin Mester.
  p. cm. — (Outstanding dissertations in linguistics)
  Thesis (Ph.D.)—University of Massachusetts, 1986.
  Bibliography: p.
  ISBN 0-8240-5192-0
  1. Grammar, Comparative and general—Phonology. 2. Morphemics. 3. Javanese language—Morphemics. 4. Grammar, Comparative and general—Reduplication. I. Title. II. Series.
  P217.3.M47 1988
  414—dc19   88-16510

Printed on acid-free, 250-year-life paper
Manufactured in the United States of America

ACKNOWLEDGEMENTS

I would like to thank my committee members: Alan Prince, John McCarthy, Lisa Selkirk, and Mark Feinstein, for their help and encouragement. I enjoyed the discussions with Mark Feinstein, whose comments and criticisms have led to many improvements. Lisa Selkirk has been an inspiring teacher, and during my stay at UMass and in particular while writing this thesis I have benefitted immensely from being able to work with her. Without John McCarthy and Alan Prince, I would never have entered the field of phonology. John McCarthy, who taught my first phonology class and was back in time at UMass to serve on my committee, contributed in many ways to this thesis, guiding my ideas towards theoretically interesting questions. To my advisor Alan Prince I owe a special debt of gratitude. He has been a constant source of inspiration throughout my graduate studies, and most of the ideas in this thesis have taken shape in discussions with him.

Many thanks also to the UMass students and faculty, in particular to Emmon Bach, Toni Borowsky, Roger Higgins, and Scott Myers, for helpful discussions on various topics. I am especially grateful to Junko Itô for discussions on virtually every aspect of this thesis and for constant moral support.

TABLE OF CONTENTS

INTRODUCTION 1

CHAPTER I. DEPENDENT TIER ORDERING AND THE OCP

    1.0   Introduction 4

    1.1   Tier Ordering 13

            1.1.1   Universal tier ordering
            1.1.1.1   Popapean labials 21
            1.1.1.2   Alur coronals 27

            1.1.2   Parametric tier ordering
            1.1.2.1   Ngbaka 32
            1.1.2.2   Ainu 46

            1.1.3   Direct core linking versus
                       dependent ordering 52

    1.2   Fusion and Spreading in Harmony Systems .. 63

            1.2.1   Height-stratified harmony 64

            1.2.2   On the scope of fusional
                       and spreading harmony 73

            1.2.3   Kirghiz dependent rounding
                       harmony 77

CHAPTER II. THE CONSONANTISM OF JAVANESE MORPHEMES:
               - A CASE STUDY -

    2.0   Introduction 86

    2.1   The Javanese Root Constraints 92
         -the empirical basis-

2.2   Directional Association and Spreading 99

2.3   OCP-interactions of Primary Articulator Features

    2.3.1   Nasality and voicing as
           dependent tiers................. 103

    2.3.2   Palatals: Continuancy as
           a dependent tier................ 105

    2.3.3   Coronals and retroflexion....... 109

    2.3.4   Root-final consonants........... 113

2.4   The Representation of Exceptional Forms... 119

2.5   Branching Prohibitions and
      Geminate Minimization..................... 122

2.6   Summary and Concluding Remarks............ 133

2.7   Appendix: Cooccurrence statistics
               for Javanese consonants........ 139

    2.7.1   Labials......................... 142
    2.7.2   Palatals........................ 144
    2.7.3   Velars.......................... 146
    2.7.4   Coronal obstruents.............. 147
    2.7.5   Combinations involving the
           root-final position........ 148
    2.7.6   Liquids......................... 153
    2.7.7   Retroflex stops and /r/......... 160
    2.7.8   Coronal/palatal cooccurrences... 162

CHAPTER III.   MELODY ASSOCIATION IN REDUPLICATION

3.0   Introduction 165

3.1   Rule Overapplication 178

    3.1.1   Dakota 186
    3.1.2   Sanskrit 190
    3.1.3   Madurese 197
    3.1.4   Chumash 200
    3.1.5   Kihehe 207

3.2	Rule Underapplication		214
	3.2.1	Missing linear context	217
	3.2.1.1	Chumash	218
	3.2.1.2	Luiseño	220
	3.2.2	Geminate blocking	225
3.3	Further Single Melody Effects: Sanskrit Deaspiration		241
3.4	Post-conflational Rules		248
3.5	Conclusion		253

BIBLIOGRAPHY 255

INTRODUCTION

   This dissertation examines a number of issues arising in multitiered nonlinear phonology in the light of the Obligatory Contour Principle (OCP) (Leben 1973, McCarthy 1979, 1981, 1986), which prohibits adjacent identical elements at the melodic level. The OCP is the formal reflex of a general strategy to analyze (partial) identity of segments as multiple association of a single melodic complex and not as a melodic sequence of identicals.

   Multiple association of individual features or of a subset of a segment's features is found in processes of partial assimilation. A number of researchers (Goldsmith 1979, 1981, Halle and Vergnaud 1980, Steriade 1982, Tuller 1981, Clements 1985, and Hayes 1986) have convincingly argued that such processes are optimally captured by rules spreading (and not copying) a certain feature from one segment into a neighboring segment, thereby creating a multiply linked structure. The important point is that a spreading analysis of partial assimilation presupposes an articulated tier structure: In order for a certain feature of a given segment to be able to spread separately from all the other features contained in the segment, the spreading feature must be representationally autonomous.

One goal of this dissertation is to provide another kind of evidence for segment-internal tier articulation. Taking the OCP as a guiding principle, we will argue that feature-sized cooccurrence restrictions can be understood as OCP-effects if the internal feature composition of segments is organized into a number of separate tiers. We will pursue the idea put forth in McCarthy (1985) that each such tier is governed by the OCP and develop a theory of tier structure which crucially posits dependencies between feature tiers. Morpheme structure constraints and harmony processes in a number of typologically diverse languages will be shown to provide evidence for a parametrized theory of dependent tier ordering. In particular, this theory will be applied to the extensive system of root consonant cooccurrence restrictions found in the Western Austronesian language Javanese (Uhlenbeck 1949).

If identity is to be represented as multiple association, copying as a phonological operation should be highly disfavored, and in nonlinear analyses spreading rules have indeed taken the place of copying rules. We will deal with one major area of phonological theory where copying of melodic units still plays a role, namely the theory of reduplication (Marantz 1982). Focussing on the proper treatment of melody association in reduplicative constructions and building on earlier nonconcatenative approaches to reduplication, we will argue that reduplicative templates are skeletal morphemes simultaneous with the root skeleton which are directly associated with the root melody and linearized by the independently necessary principle of Tier Conflation. Reduplicative constructions are thus characterized by single melodies associated with two simultaneous skeleta. This single-melody theory of reduplication does not need a reduplication-specific copying operation, and it will be shown to be empirically superior to the copying theory in that it solves some longstanding problems concerning the interaction of phonological rules with reduplication.

CHAPTER I

DEPENDENT TIER ORDERING AND THE OCP

1.0 Introduction

In this chapter I will investigate the internal structure of the segmental melody in multitiered phonology. I will approach the issue through the study of two widespread kinds of phenomena -- root structure constraints and harmony systems -- which can shed light on a number of central questions regarding the microstructure of the melody and the geometrical properties of tier structure. I will be arguing for tier separation and dependent tier ordering, with the overall goal of maximizing the explanatory role of the Obligatory Contour Principle (OCP).

It is a familiar fact that many languages impose rigorous constraints on the phonetic shape of their morphemes, constraints that are not reducible to conditions on syllable structure. What is typically ruled out is the multiple instantiation of a certain phonetic property or complex of phonetic properties inside a morpheme. For example, it is a wellknown characteristic of Japanese morpheme structure (see Itô and Mester 1986 for a recent analysis) that native morphemes cannot contain more than one voiced obstruent. Thus <u>kaze</u> 'wind' and <u>geta</u> 'Japanese

sandal' are wellformed morphemes, but forms like *gaze
or *geda violate the Voicing Constraint and are
systematically absent from the native vocabulary. The
primary domain of such constraints is the class of root
morphemes, and I will from now on refer to them as 'root
constraints'.

Our central hypothesis is that morpheme-internal
feature cooccurrence restrictions of this kind are derived
from the Obligatory Contour Principle (OCP), which is given
in (1).

(1) Adjacent autosegments on an autosegmental tier cannot
be identical.

When the OCP was first proposed by Leben (1973) (the
name of the principle is due to Goldsmith 1976), its
intended applications were prosodic features like tone.
Thus in Leben's (1973) analysis the OCP served to explain
systematic restrictions found in the tonal shapes of Mende
morphemes. In the work of McCarthy (1979, 1981)
Autosegmental Theory was extended into the traditional
domain of segmental phonology, and concomitantly the OCP
acquired a broader range of applications, it was no longer
restricted to 'suprasegmental' features. A major result
of McCarthy's work on Semitic was the fact that some of
the systematic restrictions on consonant patterns in

Semitic roots documented by Greenberg (1960) could be explained as automatic consequences of the OCP. A striking fact about verbal forms in Semitic languages is the asymmetric distribution of identical consonants. In a triconsonantal verbal form the first two consonants cannot be identical (*sasam), but the last two consonants can (samam 'poison'). This restriction was wellknown in the Arab linguistic tradition. In McCarthy's approach consonantal and vocalic (morphemic) melodies are autosegmentally autonomous with repect to each other and to the prosodic template (the skeleton). Furthermore spreading of melody elements to unfilled skeleton slots is exclusively rightward in Semitic languages and takes place after one-to-one left-to-right association of melody to skeleton. Given these independently motivated properties of Semitic morphology and phonology, McCarthy (1979, 1981) showed that the OCP directly derives the asymmetry mentioned above. To yield a verbal form like *sasam, a consonantal root ssm would have to be posited, but such a form violates the OCP. The form samam, on the other hand, results from the biconsonantal root sm, with rightward spreading of the last root consonant. Notice that the OCP explanation for the asymmetry is inextricably linked to very specific properties of the underlying phonological representation, it is by no means applicable to the string of segments as it appears on the surface.

Root constraints are often not segment-sized, but feature-sized, like the Japanese Voicing Restriction mentioned above, or they concern certain groups of features. In this light the hypothesis that all root constraints are ultimately manifestations of the OCP has far-reaching consequences for the representation of the segmental melody, requiring a more finely grained internal structure for melody elements than traditionally assumed. Individual features which are governed by root constraints must be visible for the OCP and hence occupy separate tiers: OCP-visibility implies tier autonomy.

Assigning individual features to separate tiers is compatible with a vast number of geometrical arrangements. I will argue that certain types of cooccurrence restrictions give evidence for dependent tier ordering. What is intended by the term dependent tier ordering is best illustrated by an example. A hierarchical organization is imposed on the set of features so that the vocalic features might be arranged as in (2).

(2)
```
        [round]
          |
         [back]
          |
        [high]
          |
```

Individual features, while occupying separate tiers, are not entirely autonomous and are dependent on other tiers which have a more central location.[1]

This model of dependent feature tiers is to be contrasted with a model in which the connections between the tiers are not direct, as in (2), but mediated through some other node as in (3).[2]

(3)
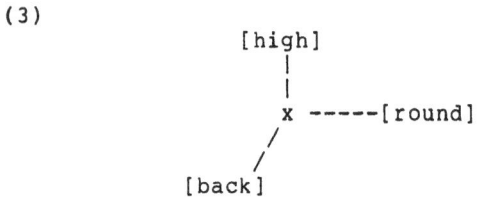

It should be noted that the nature of the mediating node which is represented as x in (3) is not at issue here. What is being contrasted in (2) and (3) is the direct versus indirect connection between the individual vowel feature tiers. I will argue that cooccurrence restrictions which involve two or more features can be understood as

---

[1] Such dependently ordered models have been proposed by several researchers (see e.g. Steriade 1982, McCarthy 1983, Archangeli 1985). However, to my knowledge, the OCP-entailments of such models have not been fully explored. Segment-internal dependency relations have also been posited, in a different way and with different motivations, in the framework of Dependency Phonology (see e.g. Anderson and Jones 1974, 1977 and Ewen 1982).

[2] A version of such a model has been called the "Independent Linking Hypothesis" in Steriade (1982).

OCP-entailments of a dependently ordered tier structure such as the one given in (2).

A typical two-feature cooccurrence restriction (a simplified version of the Ngbaka system discussed below in section 1.1.1) is given in (4).

(4)   A <u>high</u> front vowel and a <u>high</u> back vowel do not
          cooccur, and a <u>nonhigh</u> front vowel and a <u>nonhigh</u>
          back vowel do not cooccur. Otherwise, front
          and back vowels cooccur freely.

Suppose the features [high] and [back] are represented on separate tiers, with the [high] tier occupying a more central position and the [back] tier anchoring in the [high] tier. In such a situation, I will call the [back] tier the <u>dependent</u> tier and the [high] tier the <u>head</u> tier.

(5)
                    [back]   (dependent tier)
                      |
                    [high]   (head tier)
                      |

Each of the tiers is individually subject to the OCP. Under this assumption, the representation of <u>uCu</u> cannot be that given in (6), since it violates the OCP on both tiers.

(6)
```
        BACK TIER:  [+bk]   [+bk]   -->  OCP-violation
                      |       |
        HIGH TIER:  [+hi]   [+hi]   -->  OCP-violation
                      |       |
                      V   C   V
```

This does not mean, however, that <u>uCu</u> (or any other sequences of identical vowels) is impossible, since there is the alternative structure (7), where the feature on the head tier is linked to two skeleton positions.

(7)
```
                          [+bk]
                            |
                          [+hi]
                          / \
                         /   \
                        V  C  V
```

The representation for <u>uCo</u> in (8) is also ruled out, since it violates the OCP on the dependent tier while respecting it on the head tier.

(8)
```
                      [+bk] [+bk]   -->  OCP-violation
                        |     |
                      [+hi] [-hi]
                        |     |
                        V  C  V
```

Given the possibilities of multiple linking, this does not mean that successive vowels cannot agree in backness, because the structure in (9) with a single backness feature linked to two height features is available to represent uCo.

(9)
$$\begin{array}{c} [+bk] \\ / \ \backslash \\ [+hi] \ [-hi] \\ | \quad | \\ V \ \ C \ \ V \end{array}$$

In (6), where the OCP-violation occurs on both the head tier and the dependent tier, and in (8), where it occurs on the dependent tier, it has been possible to find another well-formed representation (i.e. (7) and (9) respectively) which conforms to the OCP by multiple-linking from a single feature. However, an interesting situation arises in a dependency system when the OCP is violated only on the head tier, as in the representation for uCi in (10).

(10)
$$\begin{array}{c} [+bk] \ [-bk] \\ | \quad \quad | \\ [+hi] \ [+hi] \ \dashrightarrow \ \text{OCP-violation} \\ | \quad \quad | \\ V \ \ C \ \ V \end{array}$$

Fusing the identical [+high] autosegments as in (11) circumvents the OCP violation, but the result is a contour vowel phoneme (the short diphthong ui) linked to two skeleton slots.

(11)
```
        [+bk]   [-bk]
           \   /
          [+hi]
          /   \
         V  C  V
```

The structure in (11) does not represent uCi, it represents uiCui. Since the backness tier communicates with the skeleton only through the height tier, the representation in (11) does not assign [+back] to the first V and [-back] to the second V. In fact, there is no wellformed representation for uCi in this dependency system. Besides uCi, the same considerations hold for the other [+high] sequence iCu, and the [-high] sequences oCe and eCo. Their relevant structures either violate the OCP on the height tier as in (10) or represent short diphthongs as in (11).

Thus in this dependency system, all combinations of vowels with equal height are ruled out unless the vowels also agree in backness (cf. (7)). Notice that we have actually arrived at the system of cooccurrence restrictions informally stated in (4). Root constraints of this kind, which were hitherto a collection of essentially arbitrary restrictions on phoneme combinations, can now be viewed as necessary consequences of the structure of the phonological representation in a language.

More generally, in a tier dependency system the OCP

entails the statement in (12) for elements which are adjacent (modulo tier separation).

(12)
    If two elements have identical feature representations on an autosegmental tier t, they must also have identical feature representations on all tiers dependent on t.

In this way the OCP derives syntagmatic constraints on melodies from the microstructure of melody elements.

1.1 Tier Ordering

The model of tier structure that I adopt can be considered a version of the Melody Plane Hypothesis argued for by many researchers, most notably Steriade (1982), Archangeli (1985), Clements (1985) and McCarthy (1985).

All features occupy a common melody plane which is connected to the skeleton as a whole. Only 'true' autosegments like tone are directly linked to the skeleton.[1]

---

[1] For tone this is well supported by phenomena like tonal stability and also by the minimal interaction between tone and 'segmental' features.

For example, the segment d̲ will receive the representation in (1).

(1)

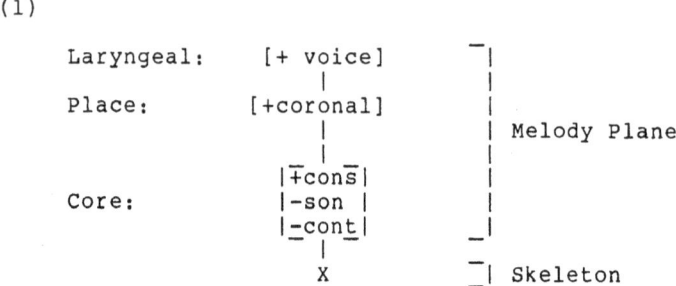

I follow McCarthy (1985) in assuming that the 'basis' of a melody element is its melodic core, occupied by the manner features [consonantal, sonorant, continuant]. Only the core is linked to the skeleton, and it corresponds to the root node in Clements (1985). As argued by McCarthy (1985), the melodic core serves several functions. It gives formal expression to the status of melodic feature ensembles as units independent of their skeletal affiliation, as is necessary for spreading and for association in reduplication. Secondly the features in the core are themselves not subject to nonlocal harmony.

The inclusion of the melodic core in a tier structure like (1) above raises some representational issues which have to be resolved before we can proceed. As a mediator between the articulator tiers and the skeleton, the melodic core constitutes an additional level of structure and causes ambiguities for the representation of geminates. Note that if nothing else is said, geminates now have two possible representations, namely (2a) and (2b). In the first case, we are dealing with a single melodic core linked to two skeleton positions, in the second case with a single place feature linked to two core units which are each separately linked to skeletal C's. Both represent morpheme-internal geminate p.

(2)
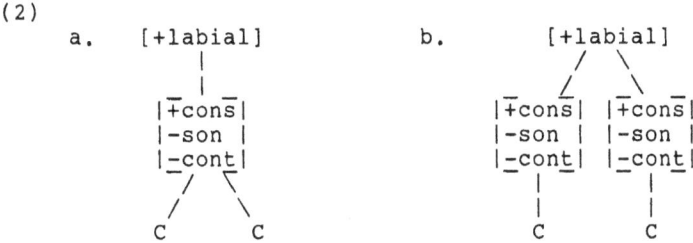

The problem here is that (2b) is not ruled out by the OCP because the core, a 'structural' tier like the skeleton, is immune to the OCP. If the core were subject to the OCP, a cluster like kt could not exist, with different place features but sharing all manner features. The cluster kt must have a representation like (3).

(3)

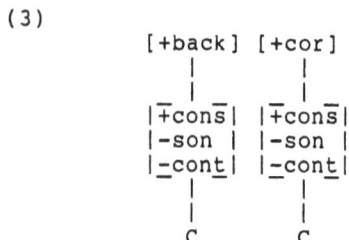

For geminates this means that the theory makes both structures in (2) available. Such a structural ambiguity of geminates is undesirable because there is no evidence that languages distinguish between two different kinds of geminates in a way which could support a representational contrast like (2a) vs. (2b). It is easy to imagine how such a hidden structural difference could be brought out by different phonological behavior of the two types of geminates. For example, in (2b) one of the core units of the two-core geminate could undergo a rule affecting the melodic core directly, whereas the other core unit would remain unaffected. This possibility could not arise for the monocore geminate in (2a). Or a rule applying only to a multiply linked [labial] feature would affect (2b), but not (2a), where [labial] is singly linked. Cases of this kind have not been reported, and therefore the representational contrast in (2) does not seem to be called for by the facts about geminates. The reasoning here from noninstantiated potential contrasts is quite parallel to McCarthy's (1986, 255) argumentation against a markedness interpretation of the OCP. McCarthy observes that if for a given segment S both multiply linked S and the sequence SS (singly linked) were in principle possible inside morphemes, with the latter just being less popular, we would open up possibilities of differential phonological behavior which never seem to be realized.

In view of these considerations, it appears imperative to restrict the representational potential of the theory in a way which makes geminates unambiguous. I will adopt a general principle requiring a strictly monomelodic representation for (total) geminates which is formulated in (4):

(4)
Geminate Minimization Principle

Melodic structures of the form (i) are illformed, where $core_x$ and $core_y$ are identical core configurations sharing all external feature specifications.

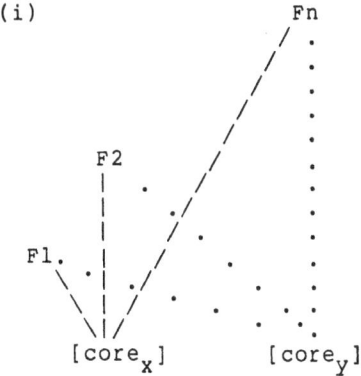

Principle (4) requires minimization of geminate structures and is in certain ways reminiscent of Steriade's (1982) Shared Feature Convention. The main empirical consequence of (4) is that it enforces branching from the core as against branching from the place feature to identical core units. Principle (4) thus resolves the representational ambiguity in favor of (5a).

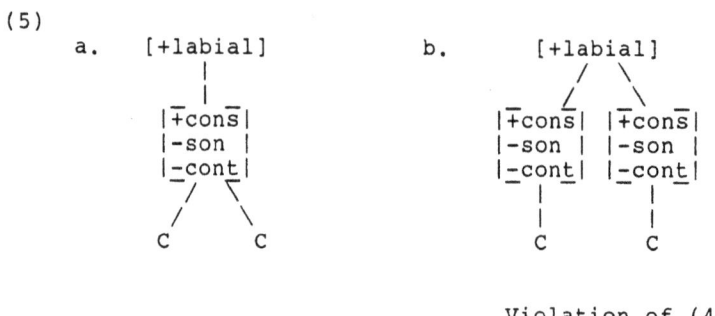

Violation of (4)

Some important consequences of the Geminate Minimization Principle (4) will appear below.

A central aspect of our model of tier structure is the assumption that the melody plane contains hierachical structure which is defined between the feature tiers themselves. With respect to the possible ordering relations between tiers, our hypothesis is that there are both universal tier orderings and tier orderings which are subject to parametric variation. It is reasonable to assume that secondary articulation features like pharyngealization and labialization are universally dependent on the primary articulator tiers, and we do not expect the reverse ordering with primary articulators dependent on secondary articulators. As will be seen below, this seems to be borne out by the facts.

On the other hand, reversals of tier ordering are possible among the vowel features. It is not the case, for example, that one vowel feature such as [high] can be considered intrinsically closer to the core than another feature such as [back] (although this ordering may be the unmarked case). We will see that the tier configurations of these features show variation, and either one may be dependent on the other.

Another case of variation is the geometrical locus of laryngeal features and of the nasal feature. These features can be dependent on the place features (see chapter II) or be directly linked to the core (see section 1.1.1).

There are thus two ways in which tier ordering can vary. When two features are equal in status (as in the case of vowel features), the ordering of the two tiers can be reversed, such that tier x can be dependent on tier y and vice versa. Besides such a reversal of dependency relations, tier ordering can also vary in that dependency structure can contrast with the absence of dependency structure: A feature occupying a dependent tier in one language may be directly linked to the core in another language and hence be independent of the behavior of other feature tiers. This kind of variation is found in the case of voicing and nasality, and it constitutes a second possibility for vowel features.

Our hypothesis is that these are the only two kinds of parametric tier ordering. Some more possibilities might have to be admitted, but it is essential to impose strict limits on the range of variation. If tiers could be arranged freely, the number of possible orderings would be astronomic, and most of these orderings would never be instantiated in natural languages.

In what follows we will first consider dependency systems which involve primary and secondary articulators. These are instances of universal tier ordering, according to our hypothesis. The velarization of Ponapean labials and the distributed/nondistributed distinction among Alur coronals will show clear dependent ordering between primary and secondary articulation, while no dependency is observed with other tiers such as nasality and voicing. We will then consider the parametric dependency systems of the vowel features in Ngbaka and Ainu. It will be argued that the differences between the two cases can be appropriately characterized by differential ordering of the [back] and [high] tiers.

1.1.1 Universal Tier Ordering

1.1.1.1 Ponapean labials

The Micronesian language Ponapean, as described in Rehg and Sohl (1981), shows a tier dependency effect involving the primary articulator feature [labial] and the secondary articulator feature [back]. Ponapean distinguishes plain labials $\underline{p}$ $\underline{m}$ and velarized labials $\underline{p^w}$ $\underline{m^w}$. According to Rehg and Sohl (1981, 44-6), these four different labial segments do not cooccur freely in morphemes. Plain and velarized labials cannot be mixed in a morpheme, either all labials in a morpheme are velarized, or none is. So we have what we might call morpheme-level velarization harmony for labials.[2]

Table (6) presents a list of morphemes with several labials (all examples from Rehg and Sohl 1981).

---

[2] In one respect, this statement goes beyond what Rehg and Sohl (1981) say. They state that $\underline{m}$ and $\underline{m^w}$ exclude each other within morphemes and likewise $\underline{p}$ and $\underline{p^w}$, but nothing is said about the combinations $\underline{p} + \underline{m^w}$ and $\underline{m} + \underline{p^w}$. However, a search of the grammar did not turn up any tautomorphemic cooccurrences of the latter kind, so the stronger statement given in the text seems warranted. There is one form $\underline{kamadip^w}$ 'feast' with a cooccurrence of $\underline{m}$ and $\underline{p^w}$, but this is almost certainly a compound ($\underline{dip^w}$ 'clan', $\underline{kama}$?).

(6)

p + p	paip	'boulder'	
	pap	'swim'	
m + m	mem	'sweet'	
	kamam	'to enjoy kava'	
p + m	parem	'nipa palm'	
	madep	'species of sea cucumber'	
$p^w + p^w$	$p^w u p^w$	'to fall'	
	$p^w o p^w e$	'shoulder'	
$m^w + m^w$	$sum^w um^w$	'trochus'	
	$kam^w am^w$	'to exhaust'	
	$m^w aam^w$	'fish'	
$m^w + p^w$	$m^w o p^w$	'out of breath'	

In all these forms velarization affects either all labials in a morpheme or none of them; velarized and nonvelarized labials do not cooccur.

Agreement in velarization holds for the whole domain of a morpheme, a different consonant intervening between two labials like r in parem or d in madep does not render the constraint inoperative.

It should be noted that velarization harmony is a strictly morpheme-internal phenomenon. Across morpheme boundary, velarized and plain labials can freely cooccur, as shown in (7).[3]

(7)
    lap^{w}ad - peseng   'to untie apart'
    paa - p^{w}oad   'four long objects'

Our hypothesis is that the feature [labial] and the feature [back] (characterizing velarization as a secondary articulation) are geometrically arranged as in (8), with [back] dependent on [labial].

(8)
```
        back
         |
        labial
         |
        [core]
```

Given this geometry, the OCP requires that morphemes with several labials be represented with a single [labial] feature. The tier structure in (8) then immediately derives the morpheme-internal velarization harmony of Ponapean as a tier dependency effect: The single [labial] feature can carry a secondary [back] specification, then all labials contained in the morpheme will surface with

---

[3]There is one local assimilation process causing labials adjacent across morpheme boundary to agree in velarization (determined by the second labial), see Itô (1986) for discussion.

labialization, as in (9a) p^{w}up^w. Or the [labial] feature does not carry such a specification, then all labials contained in the morpheme will appear without labialization, as in (9b) pap.[4] These are the only two possibilities, given the dependent tier ordering and the OCP, and the representation (9c), with mixing of velarized and plain labials, is ruled out.

(9)

```
      a.   back         b.                c.   back
           |                                    |
           lab               lab           *    lab    lab
           |                 |                  |      |
           [core]            [core]             [core][core]
           / \               / \                |      |
           C u C             C a C              C  a   C

           p^wup^w 'to fall'  pap 'to swim'    *p^wap
```

Strictly speaking, all of this holds only when two labials are adjacent (across a vowel). To complete the analysis and to account for the fact that velarization harmony is enforced across different intervening consonants, we can assume that the feature [labial] occupies a tier by itself, separate from other primary articulator features like [coronal]. Such a separation

---

[4] I am assuming that plain labials are underspecified for backness and also that nonlabials do not carry the feature specification [-labial]. Since the positive feature values are the only ones present in morpheme structure, I will write e.g. [labial] instead of [+labial]. For recent proposals on Underspecification theory see e.g. Kiparsky (1982) and Archangeli (1984).

of primary articulator tiers, which leads to long-distance OCP effects, has been argued for by McCarthy (1985) on the basis of the Semitic root structure constraints. We will return to the exact details which the analysis of such long-distance phenomena involves in the next chapter, where I present similar evidence found in the extensive system of cooccurrence restrictions governing morphemes in the Western Austronesian language Javanese.

The fact that tautomorphemic labials in Ponapean have to agree in labialization does not mean that they always have to be totally identical. As is often the case, nasality behaves as an independent articulatory parameter. Thus, p and m as well as p^w and m^w are allowed to cooccur in Ponapean morphemes (cf. parem 'nipa palm', madep 'species of sea cucumber', and $m^w op^w$ 'out of breath' in (6)). In the present framework this means that in Ponapean the nasal feature is not dependent on the place features, but rather independently linked to the core. The tier structure of Ponapean labials is therefore more fully that given in (10).

(10)
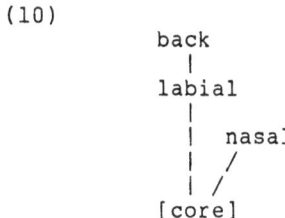

The structure for m^wop^w 'out of breath' is given in (11).

(11)
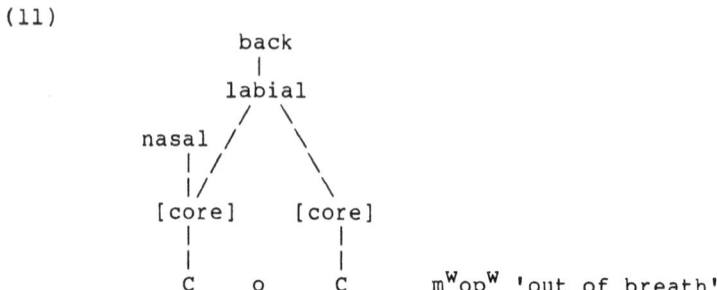
m^wop^w 'out of breath'

Notice that this structure does not violate the Geminate Minimization Principle (4) because the two consonantal core configurations do not share all melodic features. The nasal feature is linked to the first but not to the second core. If the nasal feature is linked to both cores, as in (12), Geminate Minimization is violated because the melodic cores now share all melodic features.

(12)
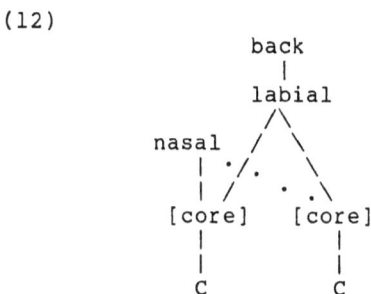

The correct representation for such a double nasal (as e.g. in m^{W}aam^W 'fish') is shown in (13), where a single melodic core carrying all the melodic information is doubly linked to two skeleton slots.

(13)
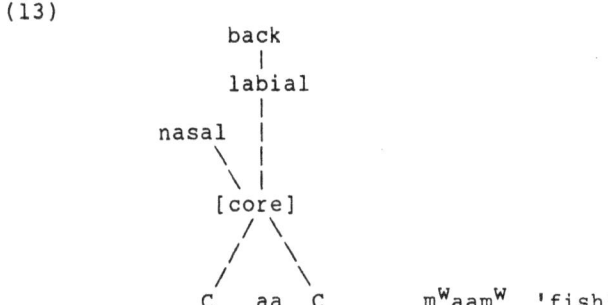

m^{W}aam^W 'fish'

1.1.1.2 Alur coronals

Summarizing results of a study of the Northeast Congo language Alur by Burssens (1969), Tucker (1969, 126) mentions the following restriction on possible root shapes:

> "[...] the alveolar plosives t and d and interdental plosives (written th and dh) are mutually exclusive in CVC roots, i.e. words such as dhetho and thedho are possible, as are words such as tado and tato, but roots of the type dh-t, th-d, t-dh, t-th, etc. are not. This situation exsists in Luo and Shilluk as well [...]."

This is again a tier dependency effect, under the assumption that the feature [distributed] which distinguishes interdentals and alveolars is a secondary feature linked to the primary place feature [coronal], as indicated in (14).

(14)
```
      dist
       |
    coronal
       |
     [core]
```

The OCP requires that morphemes containing more than one coronal plosive on the surface be underlyingly represented with a single occurrence of the feature [coronal]. Given the tier structure in (14), the root-internal [distributed] harmony for coronals then follows as a dependency effect. Since coronals differing in voicing can cooccur in a root (e.g. thadh-o) voicing must be independently linked to the core. The full melody structure of Alur coronals is shown in (15).

(15)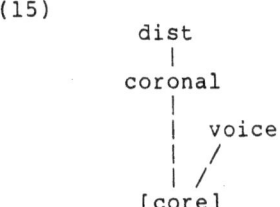

The structures in (16) illustrate how the attested combinations can be represented.

(16)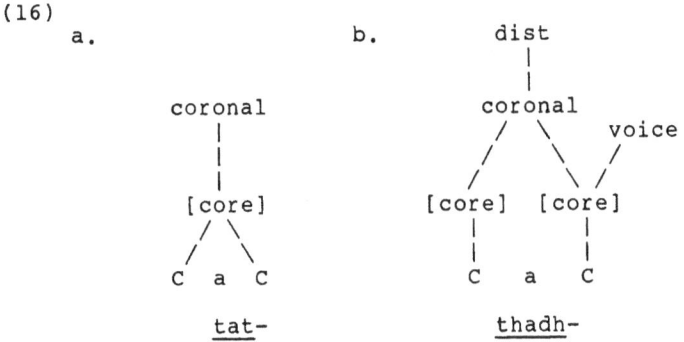

Notice that if [distributed] was not dependent on [coronal] but instead directly linked to the core, ungrammatical forms such as *tatho would be possible, as shown in (17), where the structure is in compliance with the OCP and the Principle of Geminate Minimization.

(17)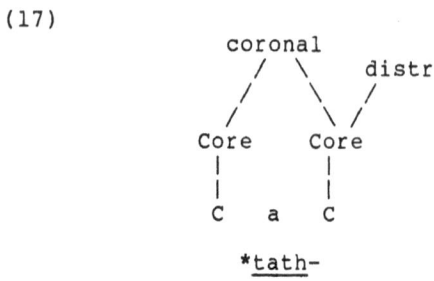

*tath-

Thus our hypothesis that the [distributed] tier is dependent on the [coronal] tier (cf. (15)) is crucial in explaining the ungrammaticality of such forms.

The melodic tier structures for Ponapean labials and Alur coronals repeated below show secondary articulation being dependent on primary articulation, and the nasal and voicing features being directly linked to the melodic core.

(18) a. Ponapean   b. Alur

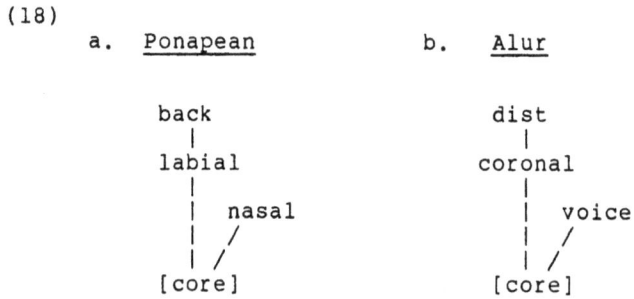

Let us consider how much of these structures is universal. The evidence from the Javanese root structure constraints in chapter II shows that nasality and voicing are not universally core-linked but can also function as place-dependent features. This raises the question whether we should always allow tiers which are dependent on the primary articulators to also have the parametric option of being linked directly to the core. If we admitted this amount of flexibility into the theory, the secondary features [back] and [distributed] could also be directly linked to the core, instead of being dependent on the place features. In particular, the following tier structures would be possible, where nasality and voicing are place-dependent and the secondary features [back] and [distributed] directly linked to the core.

(19)

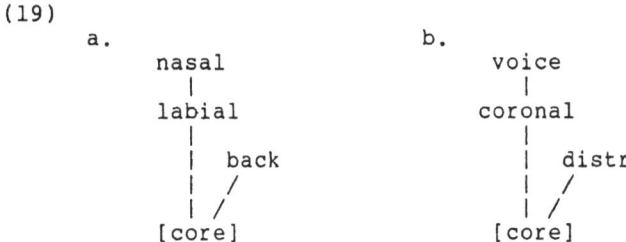

It is unlikely that tier structures of this kind are ever instantiated in natural languages and, more generally, that any cases exist where secondary articulation features must be directly linked to the core. It seems, therefore, that we can maintain the hypothesis that the dependent ordering between primary and secondary articulator tiers is universal and not subject to parametric variation.

1.1.2 Parametric Tier Ordering

In this section, the vowel systems and vowel cooccurrence restrictions of Ngbaka (1.1.2.1) and Ainu (1.1.2.2) will be contrasted, and it will be concluded that the difference between the two systems is adequately captured in a tier dependency framework if the relative ordering of the vowel features [high] and [back] is parametrized in such a way that either can be dependent on the other.

1.1.2.1 Ngbaka

Dependent tier ordering, together with the OCP, can explain the rather complex restrictions on root vowel cooccurrences found in Ngbaka, a language of the Eastern branch of the Congo-Kordofanian family. The Ngbaka facts have attracted a certain amount of attention since they were first reported by Thomas (1963) (see Wescott 1965, Chomsky and Halle 1968, Clements 1982, Itô 1984, and Churma 1984).

Ngbaka has the vowel system in (20), where E and O stand for [-ATR] mid vowels (I follow Churma (1984) in this interpretation of the mid vowel contrast).

(20)
```
        i           u
        e           o
        E           O
            a
```

In disyllabic words the following restrictions on vowel sequences are observed (Wescott 1965):

> "If a disyllabic word contains /i/, it does not also contain /u/; if /e/, it does not also contain /O/, /E/, or /o/; if /u/, it does not also contain /i/; if/o/, it does not also contain /e/, /E/, or /O/; and if /O/, it does not also contain /E/, /e/, or /o/."

I will first illustrate in more detail which vowel combinations are excluded and which are allowed in bisyllabic Ngbaka words. All examples are taken from Thomas (1963, 1970) (tone markings suppressed).

A bisyllabic word can have two identical mid vowels (21a) or two identical high vowels (21b). However, two different mid vowels or two different high vowels cannot cooccur (21c).

(21) a. bEɲE   'coller une pièce'
          bOɲO   'cervelle'
          ʔele   'oublier'
          zoko   'beau'
      b. liki   'chauffer'
          tulu   'champignon'
      c. *beno, *benO, *bEno, *bEnO, *benE, *bOno, etc.
          *liku, *luki

The low vowel a cooccurs with any vowel, including itself (22).

(22) zimba   'chercher'
      nzale   'buffle'
      kema   'singe'
      dalE   'Acacia silvicola'
      nzambu   'pulpe de noix de palme'
      duka   'épaule'
      nzambo   'pipe'
      kola   'dette'
      kalO   'chaîne'
      kOla   'tante paternelle'
      kama   'frère ou soeur'

High and mid vowels cooccur, as shown in (23).

(23) pEpu   'vent'
      niɲE   'amusement'

sEti	'chance'
gbie	'champ'
seti	'couché'
kOpu	'gobelet'

These exclusion relations can be expressed more perspicuously by referring to a feature representation as in (24).

(24)

```
         -Back  |  +Back
            i   |    u     +High
       ---------+---------
 +ATR       e   |    o
       ---------+------      -High
 -ATR       E   |    O
       ---------+---------
                     a       +Low
```

By redundancy rule, the high vowels are [+ATR], the low vowel [-ATR, +back], and the nonlow back vowels [+round].[5] The restriction on vowel sequences can then be stated as follows:

(25)   Elements from the two classes [+high] and [-high] do not cooccur with a different element from the same class.

---

[5] While the mid and high vowels receive the feature [-low] by redundancy rule, I am assuming that they are both lexically specified for the feature [high]. This assumption is necessary for the analysis presented below.

Following an insight by Churma (1984), we can understand this as a system with height-stratified backness and height-stratified ATR harmony within morphemes, i.e. vowels of the same tongue height must agree in backness and in ATR. This accounts for all observed restrictions, and the statement itself falls out of the OCP if we assume the following tier geometry for the vowel features in Ngbaka, with consonants and vowels on different tiers.

(26)

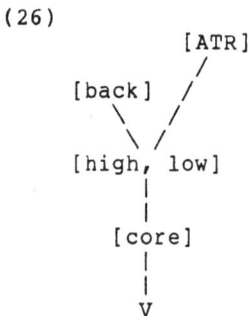

The tongue height features are represented on the most central tier, backness on a dependent tier. The feature [ATR], which is distinctive for mid vowels, is also represented on a separate dependent tier linked to the height tier. Since the mode of explanation for the feature [ATR] is exactly parallel to the backness feature, I will only discuss the latter.

Given this tier geometry, the OCP derives the Ngbaka restrictions and explains why exactly these restrictions

hold and not others. The basic idea is that all
restrictions are due to OCP conflicts on the height tier.
In particular, no morpheme-internal harmony rule or harmony
constraint has to be stipulated.

It is an important feature of the Ngbaka system that
the low vowel a can be combined with any other vowel.
This follows from the fact that the representation of a
on the height tier -- [+low] -- differs from that of
all other vowels (either [+high] or [-high]). Therefore
no OCP conflict of a with other vowels will ever arise
on the height tier. Since necessary agreement in backness
(and ATR) is induced by OCP conflicts on the height tier,
it is clear why a is the neutral element in the system.

The structures in (27) show combinations of a with
back and front vowels (to simplify the representations,
the melodic core has been suppressed).

(27)
    a.   [+bk]
                          |
             [+lo] [+hi]
              | |
            C V C V

        e.g. nzambu 'pulpe de noix de palme'

    b.   [-bk]
             |
          [-hi] [+lo]
           | |
         C V C V

        e.g. kema 'singe'

Ngbaka tolerates disharmony in backness if the vowels involved also differ in height, one being a high vowel and the other being a mid vowel. This follows because high and mid vowels have different representations on the height tier ([+high] vs. [-high]). There is no OCP conflict on the height tier, therefore no backness harmony is induced. For example, E can be combined with u:

(28)
```
        [-bk] [+bk]
          |     |
        [-hi] [+hi]
          |     |
      C   V   C   V

        e.g. pEpu   'vent'
```

A further interesting aspect of the Ngbaka system lies in the fact that there is no absolute constraint against the occurrence of two high vowels or two mid vowels in a morpheme. Such cooccurrences are permitted provided the vowels are identical.[6] We can account for the admissibility of the identity cases on principled grounds because they correspond to multiply linked structures as in (29). Since no sequences on the height tier are involved, there are also no OCP conflicts. After all,

---

[6]The importance of this fact for an explanatory account of such cooccurrence restrictions was pointed out by Itô (1984) (see Prince 1984 for general phonotactic considerations along similar lines).

a single melody element cannot enter into OCP conflicts with itself.[7]

(29)
```
        [-bk]
          |
        [+hi]
        /   \
    C  V  C  V
```
e.g. liki 'chauffer'

What is impossible in Ngbaka is a vocalism consisting of two mid vowels with different values for [back] (or [ATR]). Similarly it is impossible to have two high vowels with different values for [back] in one morpheme. Why this is so becomes clear when we inspect the representations in (30) and (31). Using the hypothetical case of a morpheme with two mid vowels differing in backness as an illustration, consider the representation (given in (30)) which such a morpheme would receive. Two different [-high] autosegments on the height tier are needed to carry the different backness features, but this is impossible, given the OCP. The case with two different high vowels in (31) is entirely parallel.

---

[7] Itô (1984) emphasizes the superiority of this account over that proposed in Clements (1982), where the admissibility of $V_i CV_i$ is stipulated by a special morpheme structure condition which takes Elsewhere Precedence over a more general morpheme structure condition which requires disharmony.

(30)
```
    *   [+bk] [-bk]
         |     |
        [-hi] [-hi]   --→  OCP-violation
         |     |
     C   V  C  V
```
*CoCe

(31)
```
    *   [-bk] [+bk]
         |     |
        [+hi] [+hi]   --→  OCP-violation
         |     |
     C   V  C  V
```
*CiCu

The OCP-based explanation for the restrictions on the vocalism of Ngbaka morphemes presupposes the segregation of consonant and vowel features onto different tiers. We might therefore expect that not only vowels, but also consonants in Ngbaka morphemes show OCP-interactions. This is indeed confirmed by the evidence. Wescott (1965), summarizing Thomas (1963), points out that consonants with the same point of articulation can by no means freely cooccur within morphemes:

> [...] if a disyllabic word contains a voiceless consonant, it does not also contain the voiced counterpart of that consonant (that is, /p/ excludes /b/, /s/ excludes /z/, etc.). Similarly, if a disyllabic word contains a voiced obstruent, it does not also contain the prenasalized counterpart of that obstruent (that is, /b/ excludes /mb/, /z/ excludes /nz/, etc);

if such a word contains a prenasalized obstruent, it does not also contain the corresponding nasal (that is, /mb/ excludes /m/, /nz/ excludes /n/, etc.) [...].

These consonant cooccurrence restrictions have the form of a gradation system as in (32), where for each place of articulation adjacent elements on a hierarchical scale "voiceless obstruent - voiced obstruent - prenasalized voiced obstruent - nasal" exclude each other, whereas nonadjacent elements are compatible.[8]

(32)
    p - b - mb - m

In the present framework we can account for these cooccurrence restrictions along the following lines. The tier structure which characterizes the Ngbaka consonant system is summarized in (33).

---

[8]There is a further restriction on cooccurrences of labials with labiovelars which will not be analyzed here.

(33)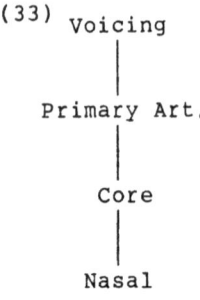

    i. The Voicing Tier is dependent on the Primary Articulator Tier. (parametric)

    ii. The Primary Articulator Tier is directly linked to the Core. (universal)

    iii. The Nasal Tier is directly linked to the Core. (parametric)

The underlying feature specifications are obviously crucial if the observed cooccurrence restrictions are to be derived from the OCP. One possibility is given in (34), taking the labial series in (32) as an example.

(34)

    p : [+lab]

    b : [+lab], [+voi], [-nas]

   mb : [+lab], [+nas,-nas]

    m : [+lab], [+nas]

Note that mb is simultaneously specified as [+nasal] and [-nasal]. Later redundancy rules specify p as [-nas, -voi], and m and mb as [+voi]. Incorporating the feature specifications in (34) into the Ngbaka tier structure yields the representations in (35) (small c represents consonantal melodic cores).

(35)

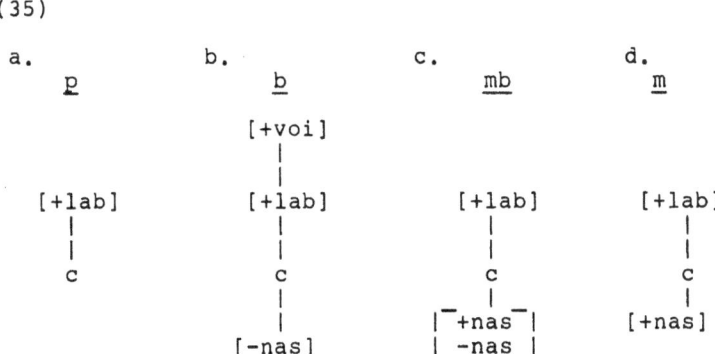

Given these structures, the OCP derives the gradational cooccurrence restrictions governing the Ngbaka consonants in the following way. As shown in (36) cooccurrences of p and b are ruled out because the dependent ordering of the voicing feature induces an OCP violation on the [labial] tier (a merged [labial] feature would carry a voicing specification and hence could not denote pb).

(36)
```
              [+voi]
               |
  *  [+lab]  [+lab]
       |       |
       c       c

       p       b
```

On the other hand, p can cooccur with mb and m because [labial] does not have to carry a differential dependent feature in these combinations and can therefore branch to the two cores, as indicated in (37). This does not violate Geminate Minimization since the two cores carry different specifications.

(37)
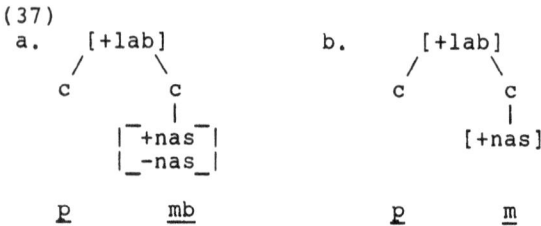

The voiced obstruent b is incompatible with mb but compatible with m, as shown in (38a,b).

(38)
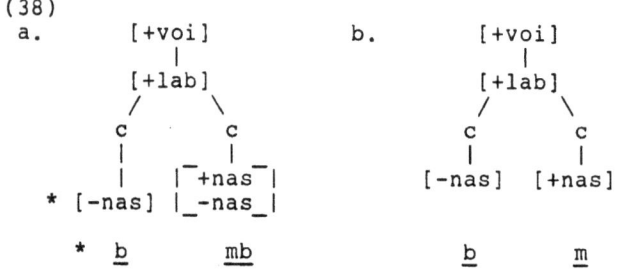

The OCP-confict in (38a) arises between the two [-nas] specifications. The assumption here is that the [-nasal] feature which is part of the nasal contour, although visible for the OCP, cannot be the head of a branching structure but is insolubly connected to its [+nasal]

partner. Note that it is crucial to regard the elements of the nasal contour as underlyingly unordered with respect to each other, otherwise the bidirectionality of the cooccurrence restriction (both *b + mb and *mb + b are excluded) would not be derivable from the OCP. For (38b) (and vacuously also for (38a)) I assume that the [+voice] specification originating in b can be accomodated by the nasal, which is underlyingly not specified for voicing.

The prenasalized obstruent mb finally is incompatible with the nasal m because of the two adjacent [+nasal] specifications, as illustrated in (39).

(39)
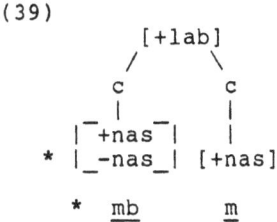

The compatibility of m with the other labials has already been demonstrated.

This brief sketch of an analysis obviously would have to be spelled out in further detail, and the underlying feature specifications necessary to trigger the OCP in the relevant cases deserve closer scrutiny, my only aim here was to indicate a way of accounting for the consonantal restrictions within the dependency framework.

1.1.2.2 Ainu

Ainu, an almost extinct language spoken in northern Japan (Hokkaido) whose genetic affiliation is unclear, has a regular dissimilation process affecting glides and certain suffixal vowels. The characteristics of the Ainu dissimilation phenomenon provide further support for the approach to root constraints proposed in this chapter and will in addition allow us to sharpen our theoretical assumptions in certain ways. For the Ainu facts and the basic analysis I am very much indebted to Itô (1984).

Ainu has a transitivizing -V suffix which is attached to roots (which are generally of the form CVC). The vocalism of this suffix (and of another -V suffix deriving possessed forms of nouns) depends in intricate ways on the vocalism of the root and displays both 'harmonic' and 'disharmonic' behavior.

For roots ending in true consonants (≠ glides), two cases have to be distinguished. In one class of roots, the suffix vowel is identical to the root vowel (40). All examples are from Chiri (1952) via Itô (1984).

(40)

mak-a	'to open'	tas-a	'to cross'
ker-e	'to touch'	per-e	'to tear'
pis-i	'to ask'	nik-i	'to fold'
pop-o	'to boil'	tom-o	'to concentrate'
tus-u	'to shake'	yup-u	'to tighten'

In a second class of roots, the suffix vowel differs from the root vowel. When the root vowel is nonlow, the suffix vowel is a high vowel opposite in backness to the root vowel (41).

(41)

hum-i	'to chop up'	mus-i	'to choke'
pok-i	'to lower'	hop-i	'to leave behind'
pir-u	'to wipe'	kir-u	'to alter'
ket-u	'to rub'	rek-u	'to ring'

When the root vowel is low, the suffix vowel can be a front or back high vowel, with the choice lexically determined (42).

(42)

kar-i	'to rotate'	sar-i	'to look back'
ram-u	'to think'	rap-u	'to flutter'

The distribution of final glides in roots is restricted by a dissimilation requirement exactly parallel to the one governing the choice of suffixal vowels. Nonlow back vowels in the root allow only the front glide y, front vowels only the back glide w. Vowel-glide dissimilations

of this kind are quite common cross-linguistically. The
low root vowel a allows both y and w, with the choice again
lexically determined. Secondly, the suffix vowel after
roots ending in glides shows no variation and is uniformly
e. Examples illustrating the possible vowel-glide
combinations appear in (43).

(43)
```
   a. poy-e    'to mix'         moy-e    'to move'
      huy-e    'to observe'     tuy-e    'to cut'

   b. hew-e    'to slant'       rew-e    'to bend'
      piw-e    'cause to run'   chiw-e   'to sting'

   c. ray-e    'to kill'        say-e    'to wind'
      chaw-e   'to solve'       taw-e    'pull with force'
```

In our analysis we can largely follow Itô's (1984)
proposal, which involves two main assumptions:

(i) Consonantal and nonconsonantal melodies are segregated
onto different tiers.

(ii) The melody element filling the suffixal V-slot or
serving as a root-final glide is part of the root melody
and subject to a dissimilation requirement. We are dealing
with a floating melody element which only appears when
a skeletal anchor is available.

To capture the dissimilation facts, Itô (1984) proposes the melodic dissimilation rule (44).

(44)
    [+high] → [-a back] / [a back] ___

The obvious move in the present context is to derive Itô's (1984) dissimilation rule (44) from the OCP. The most attractive option is to adopt the following feature structure for Ainu vowels and glides, where the feature [back] occupies a separate and more central tier on which the height tier is dependent (following Itô 1984, I assume that a is unspecified for [back]).

(45)

[+low]	[-high]	[+high]	[-high]	[+high]
[ ]	[-back]	[-back]	[+back]	[+back]
[-cons]	[-cons]	[-cons]	[-cons]	[-cons]
a	e	y,i	o	w,u

Root melodies are governed by the following constraint (46):

(46)
    A final floating [-cons] melody element must be [+high].

Since [back] occupies a separate tier on which the height tier is dependent, the OCP derives all dissimilation effects.

Because of the dependence of height on backness, it is impossible to get two successive vocalic melodies which agree in backness but differ in height (47).

(47)
```
        [-hi][+hi]      [-hi][+hi]
         |    |          |    |
      *  [+bk][+bk]    * [-bk][-bk]
         |    |          |    |
         C V C V         C V C V

         *CoCu           *CeCi
```

Agreement in backness is only possible if there is at the same time agreement in height. In that case we are dealing with a monovocalic root whose vowel melody has spread to the suffixal V slot, as illustrated in (48).

(48)
```
          [+hi]
            |
          [-bk]
          /  \
        p V s V

         pisi        'to ask'
```

The fact that glide-final roots are always followed by $\underline{e}$ is derived as in Itô's analysis. There is a general prohibition (49) against multiple linking of melody elements inside the syllable (the sequences *yi and *wu are excluded, and there are no long vowels).

(49)

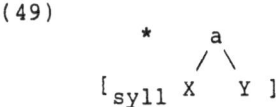
```
         *    a
             / \
    [syll  X   Y ]
```

This syllable structure constraint overrides the spreading option and makes it impossible for the root-final glide to spread to the empty V-slot, which will be filled by the default vowel e.

In this analysis, Ainu differs from Ngbaka (see section 1.1.2.1 above) in the ordering of tiers. In Ngbaka the height tier is more central, and the backness tier is dependent on it. As a consequence, we get height dissimilation effects: If two successive (nonlow) vowels in a morpheme are not identical, they must be taken from different height classes. In Ainu, the backness tier is more central, and the height tier is dependent on it. Therefore we get backness dissimilation effects: Nonidentical successive vowels in a morpheme must differ in backness. Taken together, the two analyses show that the dependency order of vowel feature tiers is open to parametric variation.

1.1.3 Direct Core Linking versus Dependent Ordering

We have seen in the preceding sections that the OCP imposes a dissimilation pattern on the head tier of a dependency structure: Adjacent melody elements disagreeing in their value for a dependent feature must also disagree in their values for the head feature, otherwise the OCP is violated on the head tier. The important result is an implication: difference in dependent features → difference in head feature (or equivalently: head feature identity → dependent feature identity). In this view, whether a certain feature dissimilates is a consequence of its position in the overall geometry of tiers (cf. the difference between Ngbaka and Ainu).

In this section I will consider an alternative approach to the vowel restrictions of Ngbaka and Ainu in which the feature tiers are not dependently ordered but are directly linked to the melodic core. In such a direct core-linking approach, the cooccurrence restrictions are captured by imposing on the dissimilating feature a branching prohibition which disallows multiple linking.[9] I will first discuss how such a direct core-linking approach works, and then show that in cases involving more

---

[9] In its crucial use of branching prohibitions this alternative account draws its inspiration from McCarthy's (1985) work on the Semitic root constraints.

than two features the direct core-linking theory is
empirically inadequate without further stipulations.

Recall that in Ngbaka two <u>different</u> high vowels and
two <u>different</u> mid vowels cannot cooccur in morphemes,
whereas <u>identical</u> high vowels and <u>identical</u> mid vowels
can cooccur. In a direct core-linking theory, the Ngbaka
vowels have the structure given in (50a). Both the Height
Tier and the Backness Tier are directly linked to the
core. (I will simplify the discussion by leaving out the
feature ATR, it behaves in all essential respects like
the backness feature.) In addition, the feature [high]
is governed by a constraint against multiple linking (50b).

(50)
    a.

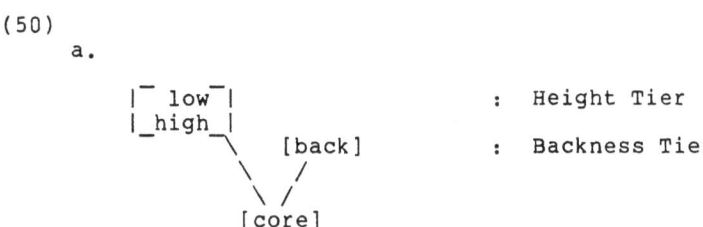

: Height Tier

: Backness Tier

    b.   * [high]

As shown in (51), (50b) rules out a vowel sequence like ui because [+high] would have to branch to two cores (or violate the OCP).

(51)
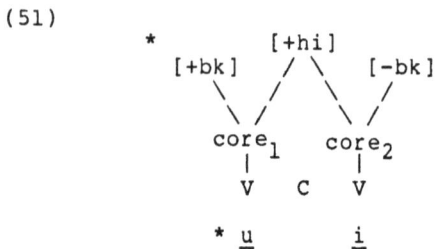

Vowels of the same height can cooccur in Ngbaka morphemes, however, if they agree in both height and backness. To account for such cooccurrences, we can rely on multiple linking of the melodic core. For example, the sequence ii is not represented as in (52a) with two separate cores to which [+high] and [-back] are doubly linked - this would violate (50b) - , but with a single core linked to two vowel slots, as in (52b). Note that (52b) does not violate (50b).

(52) a.
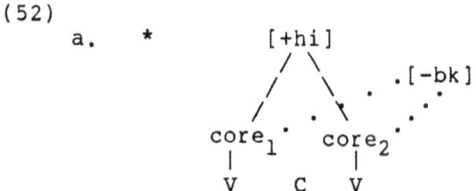

b.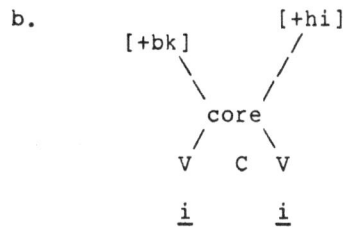

An analoguous treatment is possible for Ainu: In Ainu it is the feature [back] which dissimilates and not the feature [high], and we can express this by imposing a branching prohibition on [back] instead of on [high].

The theoretical question which has to be addressed now is the following: Can we always substitute branching prohibitions for dependent ordering, that is, is a theory which does not allow for any melody-internal structure and takes all features to be directly linked to the melodic core empirically adequate if coupled with branching prohibitions?

The Direct Core-linking theory and the Dependent Ordering Theory make different predictions once we look beyond simple situations involving only two features. Relevant evidence of this kind is found in Ngbaka, and it concerns combinations of vowels of equal height. In the Direct Core-Linking Theory, successive vowels of the same height must be represented with a single core linked to two V slots, hence they necessarily have to agree in all features which are linked to the melodic core. A closer examination of the Ngbaka facts reveals that this identity requirement is too strict. While identity in vowel height always implies identity in backness (and ATR), there is a third feature, namely nasality, which can vary independently. It appears from the data in Thomas (1963) that two successive vowels in a morpheme can be identical in all features except nasality. Two minimal pairs appear in (53).

(53)
    babã   'compagnon'   vs.   baba   'perdre'
    bañã   'chenille'   vs.   baña   'mâchoire'

With dependent tier ordering, we can capture this as follows:

(54)
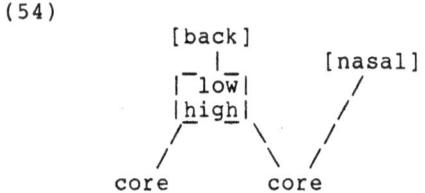

Since nasality is not part of the dependency system, it acts as an independent parameter. Height identity implies backness identity but does not imply nasalisation identity.

Cases of this kind are a problem for a theory which recognizes only independent linking to the core. In such a theory the only structure available is (55) (under the assumption that [nasal] is in fact linked to the melodic core and not to the skeleton; I will argue for this assumption below):

(55)
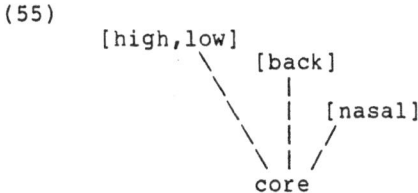

If we now impose a branching prohibition on the dissimilating feature [high], we rule out forms which are in fact well-formed. Core spreading is too coarse a tool in this case, since it implies identity in all features, including nasality. In a sense, nasality has nothing to do with the restriction, and this is not brought out in the structure. To capture the facts, it would be necessary to resort to a conditional branching prohibition which looks simultaneously at three tiers, something like "[high] is allowed to branch to core elements c_1 and c_2 only if [back] also branches to c_1 and c_2." This is an unwelcome enrichment of the theory, and a dependency which finds a direct configurational expression in the theory with dependent ordering is expressed in a roundabout way by a complex conditional statement.

This argument presupposes that the nasal specification of vowels in Ngbaka forms an integral part of the melody unit and is not directly linked to the skeleton like tonal features. Otherwise, the structure given in (56) could characterize an independently nasalized vowel.

(56)
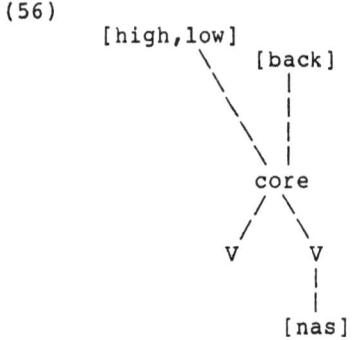

It could perhaps be argued that direct skeletal linking of nasality, as in (56), is universally ruled out, but let us here suppose, for the sake of the argument, that a structure like (56) is allowed in Universal Grammar.

A first kind of evidence against skeletal linking of nasality is found in a form of initial CV reduplication which derives verbal nouns from verb roots. This process is fully productive and applies even to French loans like ʔēdè̄ - ʔè̄ʔēdè̄ 'aider'. As illustrated in (57), the tone

of the first root vowel is not copied, but replaced by
a low tone which I interpret as the default tone of
Ngbaka. In some contexts this default low tone on the
reduplicative prefix undergoes further rules. For example,
the sequence low-high changes to mid-high, reflecting a
general prohibition in Ngbaka against high-low and low-high
sequences inside words (see Thomas 1963, 129-35 for
detailed discussion). In the following examples the
symbols ` ¯ ´ stand for low, mid, and high tone,
respectively.

(57)
    hā   hahā   'prendre'
    zīE   zizīE   'vomir'
    sūa   susūa   'taper, marteler'
    sí   sīsí   'gonfler'
    ʔálū   ʔūʔálū   'souffler'

Different from tone, nasality is preserved in
reduplication, as illustrated in (58).

(58)
    hȭ   hõhȭ   'manger'
    zẽ   zẽ̄zẽ   'se chauffer'

We can understand this reduplicative pattern as
involving copying/association of the melodic core, which

includes nasality but not tone. The prefixal vowel then receives a default low tone.

The behavior of two vowel-copying suffixes, the frequentative suffix -k$\tilde{V}$ and the resultative suffix -l$\tilde{V}$, lends further support to the view that nasality is linked to the melodic core and not to the skeleton. As is illustrated in (59), the suffixal vowel in these cases is always identical to the final vowel of the verbal root. The tone of the root vowel, however, is not preserved, and the suffix vowel always appears with low tone.

(59)
a. kpā   'couper entièrement, graser'
   kpā-kà   'gratter'
b. kōlō   'diviser'
   kōlō-kò   'hâcher'
c. tō   'taper'
   tō-lò   'frapper'
d. yū   'couler'
   yū-lù   'égoutter'

We can interpret this as linear spreading of the melodic core of a vowel melody to an unfilled V slot. The forms in (60) illustrate that nasality, different from tone, is preserved under spreading.

(60)   sĩã   'déchirer'
       sĩã-kã   'déchiqueter'

This is the expected result under the assumption that the feature [nasal] is linked to the melodic core, whereas tonal autosegments are linked to the skeleton.

Thus the behavior of vowel nasality in both reduplication and vowel spreading lends support to the hypothesis that nasality in Ngbaka is expressed in the melody plane and linked to the melodic core. If we accept this conclusion, we have an argument that a theory which allows no melody-internal structure is empirically inadequate. Dependent ordering, on the other hand, allows us to impose the necessary structure on the set of features (cf. (54)).

These considerations suggest that dependent ordering cannot be given up in favor of direct core-linking cum branching prohibitions. On the other hand, branching prohibitions cannot be entirely abolished as part of the theory since we must be able to say for example that a certain language does not have underlying geminates.

Both dependent ordering and branching prohibitions are thus independently necessary ingredients of the theory, and an important question which needs further study is whether they have strictly disjoint domains of application. One possibility is that universally invariant parts of melodic tier structure are never subject to branching prohibitions, whereas tier configurations which are established on a language-particular basis allow the linking relations between the tiers involved to be further restricted to one-to-one mapping. Thus laryngeal features, whose position in tier structure is variable in that they can anchor either in the primary articulators or in the core, can be governed by a language-particular branching prohibition (cf. for example the branching prohibition for [voice] in Itô and Mester 1986, 72). On the other hand the linking of primary articulators to the melodic core is universal, so no branching prohibition can be imposed on it. It should be noted in this context that the linking relations between the primary articulators and the core are already constrained by the universal Geminate Minimization Principle, which rules out spurious geminate representations like (61) where [labial] branches to two identical core configurations.

(61)

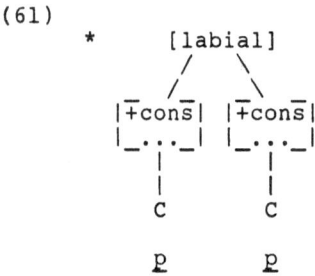

Geminate Minimization here requires a single core associated with two skeleton positions, which implies single linking of the [labial] feature.

If the linking of primary articulators to the core cannot be constrained in a language-particular way, the alternative account for the Ngbaka and Ainu cooccurrence restrictions is ruled out in principle in favor of the dependency account. Noting that it is clearly an empirical issue whether the domain of constraints against multiple linking is restricted in this way, I will assume such a limitation as a working hypothesis in this thesis.

1.2 Fusion and Spreading in Harmony Systems

In this section, I will show that a number of phenomena encountered in vowel harmony systems receive a natural explanation if we approach them from the perspective of dependent tier ordering. In section 1.2.1 it is argued that the height-stratified rounding harmony system of Yawelmani Yokuts is best understood as a manifestation of geminate-fusing Tier Conflation, applying to a dependency system of tiers. I will call this type of harmony "fusional harmony". Section 1.2.2 explores the relative empirical domains of fusional harmony and spreading harmony. Section 1.2.3 investigates the complex harmony system of Kirghiz, where fusional and spreading harmony interact.

1.2.1 <u>Height-stratified harmony</u>

The height-stratified vowel harmony system of Yawelmani Yokuts originally described in Newman (1944) has been the object of a number of analyses (Kuroda 1967, Kenstowicz and Kisseberth 1979, Archangeli 1984, 1985). The underlying vowel system of Yawelmani Yokuts is given in (1), where each vowel can be long or short.

(1)
                    i   u
                              o
                         a

Long high vowels are subject to a postlexical lowering rule which is responsible for the appearance of surface <u>e</u> and for many instances of surface <u>o</u>. As is well known, Yawelmani has a pervasive process of rounding harmony which is height-stratified in the way indicated in (2).

(2) u rounds a following i: u C₀ i --> u C₀ u

    o rounds a following a: o C₀ a --> o C₀ o

    u does not round a following a: u C₀ a -/-> u C₀ o

    o does not round a following i: o C₀ i -/-> o C₀ u

The following examples (from Newman 1944) illustrate harmonic alternations in suffixes. (The effects of two postlexical rules, Lowering and Shortening, have been suppressed in these forms in the interest of clarity; capital letters stand for retroflex consonants; page numbers refer to Newman 1944.)

(3) a. Aorist

    ʔugun-hun   'drank'   151
    c'uum-hun   'devoured'   122
      ('-> [o] by Lowering and Shortening)

    t'uy-hun   'shot'   163
    duyduy-hun   'stung rep.'   122
    duulul-hun   'climbed'   122
      ('-> [oo] by Lowering)

    ʔohyoo-hin   'search'   163
    c'ow-hin   'touched'   164

    lihim-hin   'ran'   137
    Sil'-hin   'saw'   145
    ninii-hin   'became quiet'   122
      ('-> [ee] by Lowering)

    xayaa-hin   'placed'   166
    wan-hin   'gave'   166
    caw-hIn   'shouted'   135
    ʔagay-hin   'pulled'   134
    tan-hin   'went'   134
    yawal-hin   'followed'   122

b. Dubitative

Suug-al ('→ [oo] by Lowering)	'might pull out'	120
hoTn-ol	'might take the scent'	120
di?S-al	'might make'	120
xat-al	'might eat'	120

c. Imperative

t'uy-k'a	'shoot!'	118
yolow-k'o	'assemble!'	118
xoSxoS-k^{T}o	'rub repeatedly!'	118
t'oyix-k'a	'give medicine'	118
lan-k'a	'hear!'	118

d. Passive Verbal Noun

lox-honoo	'being eaten'	149
gob-honoo	'being taken in'	22
luk'ul-hanaa	'being buried'	149
hudhud-hanaa	'being repeatedly recognized'	149

The interesting point here is that rounding disharmony is permitted if the vowels involved differ in height, but not if they have the same value for [high]. There are two tiers in the vowel feature plane, one for the feature [high] and one for the feature [round], which are aligned as in (4) (following Archangeli 1985).

(4)
```
        [round]
           |
        [high]
           |
           V
```

The [round] tier is dependent on the [high] tier and has no immediate access to the skeleton, all connections are mediated through the [high] tier.

I will assume, following Kuroda (1967) and in particular Archangeli (1984, 1985), that suffix vowels in Yokuts are unspecified for rounding. The unmarked value for the feature [round] is [-round], and this is the value which is assigned by default to vowels underlyingly unspecified for [round] unless they receive a specification in some way in the phonological derivation. I would like to suggest that the one and only way in which vowels which are unspecified for [round] receive the feature [+round] is through the action of Tier Conflation. Let us consider one of the examples given in (3) above, the aorist form t'uy-hun 'shot'. The underlying representation after affixation of the nonfuture suffix is (5), with the root vowel specified as [+round], but without rounding-specification on the suffix vowel.

(5)
```
              [+rd]
               |
              [+hi]      [+hi]
               |          |
            t'u y    +   h i n
```

Through the action of (morphemic) Tier Conflation, the vocalic melodies of root and suffix come to occupy the same tier -- this assumption seems necessary for the analysis of any vowel harmony process. It has been suggested by McCarthy (1986) that, as part of Tier Conflation, heteromorphemic identicals (i.e. geminates) are fused into a single melody element. It is not clear whether this is a universal concomitant of Tier Conflation or a separate parameter set by individual languages, I will here assume the latter.

Let us now suppose that in Yokuts Tier Conflation is accompanied by such fusion of identicals. This has interesting consequences for a melody plane which contains dependent tiers. Consider again the representation in (5) above. Both root and suffix vowel are [+high], and fusing the two [+high] autosegments into one will result in the representation given in (6).

(6)
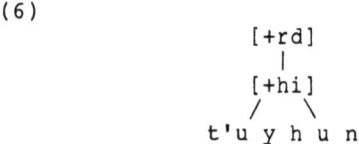

Although only the feature [+high] is directly involved in the fusion effected by Tier Conflation, the hierarchical tier structure has the consequence that the second vowel is derivatively also specified as [+round] in this case, and the default rule inserting [-round] can no longer apply.

The form hoTn-ol 'might take the scent' (from underlying /hoTn-al/) is derived in an entirely parallel fashion, the only difference being that [-high] is fused instead of [+high].

(7)
```
                    [+rd]
                      |
                    [-hi]   [-hi]
                      |       |
                    h o T n + a l
```

```
                          [+rd]
Tier Conflation             |
   cum                    [-hi]
   Fusion                 /   \
                        h o T n o l
```

The crucial advantage of this approach concerns the case of vowels which differ in height, as in c'ow-hin 'touched' (8a) and t'uy-k'a 'shoot!' (8b). The representations of these forms do not induce any fusion on the [high] tier when Tier Conflation takes place, because the two height values are different.

(8)   a.   [+rd]   b.   [+rd]
            | |
            [-hi] [+hi]   [+hi] [-hi]
            | | | |
            c'o w h i n   t'u y k a

Since in this analysis rounding harmony is a derivative effect of the fusion of identical [high] autosegments by Tier Conflation and not a process in itself, we have an immediate explanation for its absence in vowel sequences which differ in height. For a form like c'owhin the only respect in which underlying and surface representation differ is due to the operation of default [-round] insertion, which specifies the suffix vowels as unrounded (see (9)). As a result, 'rounding disharmony' is permitted in vowels differing in height.

(9)   [+rd] [-rd] ← by default
                 | |
                 [-hi] [+hi]
                 | |
                 c'o w h i n

We can make a number of general observations about this analysis. As a first result we note that there is no special rule of rounding harmony in Yokuts which would have to be constrained so as to spread [+round] in a height-stratified manner, i.e. from [+high] to [+high] and from [-high] to [-high]. Rather, Yokuts is characterized by a particular tier structure, with a more central height tier and a tier for the feature [round] which is anchored in the height tier. Tier Conflation fuses identicals on the two tiers. Since only [+round] is underlyingly specified and since suffixes are obligatorily unspecified for rounding, the crucial action of Tier Conflation takes place on the head tier, where the feature [high] is represented. Given the tier geometry with rounding dependent on height, this results in derivative rounding harmony effects. The precise nature of the harmony effects follows from the fact that Tier Conflation only fuses adjacent identicals on the height tier, therefore rounding harmony, as a derivative effect of fusion, will only appear between vowels of like height. Looking beyond Yokuts, we see that this approach provides a principled explanation for the existence of height-stratified harmony systems and the absence of harmony systems governed by height polarity (where only vowels opposite in height would show harmonic interaction). If the height-stratified character of Yokuts harmony were encoded in a special harmony rule stipulating height identity by means of a coefficient variable, we could just as well imagine a rounding harmony rule spreading rounding from [a high] to [-a high]. Such systems have not been reported, and the tier structure approach pursued here provides a principled explanation for this.

It would be logically possible to encode such a restriction in Universal Grammar by proscribing the polarity use of the alpha-notation. We would still have an inferior theory, one which needs a special exclusion clause where the theory based on dependent tier ordering and tier conflation makes the correct predictions from the start.

Furthermore we can tighten phonological theory by disallowing the use of descriptively powerful coefficient variables in (language-particular) phonological rules. Since Tier Conflation (ultimately, the OCP) detects occurrences of adjacent identical autosegments on a tier, no variable over feature coefficients is necessary to capture the fact that rounding is transmitted only from [a high] to [a high] (earlier analyses had to have recourse to such a device, see e.g. Archangeli (1985:350)). As has been argued by a number of researchers in Nonlinear Phonology (Halle and Vergnaud 1980, Steriade 1982, Hayes to appear, and others), assimilation processes are best understood as involving autosegmental spreading and not copying of features, so their statement requires no alpha-notation. In the same vein, the analysis of Yokuts rounding harmony presented above relies on operative principles which are intrinsic to the autosegmental framework (tier ordering, Tier Conflation, OCP) and does not make use of the powerful algebraic device of coefficient variables.

1.2.2 On the scope of fusional and spreading harmony

One important question which we must now address concerns the relative roles of feature fusion and feature spreading in harmony systems. In the view defended here, we are dealing with two separate mechanisms which have distinct empirical domains. Thus harmony by fusional Tier Conflation and harmony by autosegmental feature spreading, as developed in Clements (1976) and other work, complement each other and can in fact coexist in a single language (see section 1.2.3 below).

Fusional harmony is involved whenever harmony-triggers and harmony-undergoers are governed by specific similarity conditions like the equal-height requirement of Yokuts. In a tier dependency system, such conditions can be directly expressed by positing a head tier occupied by a feature shared by triggers and undergoers. In fact, no condition at all has to be stated, since the tier configuration itself embodies the condition. In the course of fusional Tier Conflation, a feature F on the dependent tier acquires an extended domain in those situations where its anchor on the head tier fuses with an identical autosegment which was previously not linked to F.

Spreading harmony is involved if there are no stratificational restrictions. Turkish vowel harmony is a case in point. Vowels in Turkish words are subject to two harmony processes. Backness harmony requires that all vowels in a word agree in their value for the feature [back], and roundness harmony requires that high vowels agree in roundness with preceding (high or nonhigh) vowels.

(10) Turkish Vowel System

i	ü	ɨ	u
e	ö	a	o

The two harmony processes are illustrated by the suffix alternations in (11) (from Clements and Sezer 1982, 216).

(11)

      -In (gen.sg.)   -lAr (nom.pl.)

      (in~ɨn~un~ün)   (ler~lar)

ip - in	'rope'	ip - ler	
kɨz - ɨn	'girl'	kɨz - lar	
yüz - ün	'face'	yüz - ler	
pul - un	'stamp'	pul - lar	
el - in	'hand'	el - ler	
sap - ɨn	'stalk'	sap - lar	
köy - ün	'village'	köy - ler	
son - un	'end'	son - lar	

Turkish has no neutral vowels, but there are lexically opaque vowels (e.g. the o̲ of the progressive suffix -Iyo̲r).

Turkish backness harmony shows no dependency effects, that is, backness harmony is independent of the other vowel features. The [back] feature is directly linked to the core with no dependent tiers, and the harmony rule is formulated in (12) as spreading of [back] to another core.

(12)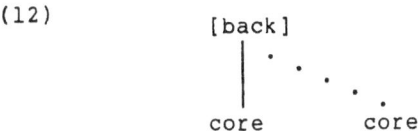

Since the consonantal and vocalic cores are linearly arranged, backness spreading defined on the melodic core also explains the harmonic interaction of palatal k̲ (Clements and Sezer 1982, 239), which induces front harmonic behavior in following vowels. Note that backness harmony cannot be accounted for by fusion, since we would have to posit a different head tier on which fusion could take place. There is no appropriate feature which could mediate between the core and [back] and still account for the consonant-vowel interactions.

Turkish rounding harmony, different from backness harmony, is height-restricted with respect to its targets, but it is not height-stratified like rounding harmony in

Yokuts. While harmonizing vowels must be [+high],[1] harmony-triggers can be both [+high] and [-high], so there is no condition of height equality on triggers and targets. Turkish rounding harmony is formulated in (13) as a rule spreading rounding rightwards onto [+high] vowels (cf. Archangeli 1985).

(13)
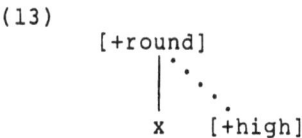

Notice that a fusional analysis is impossible here since fusion must not apply to different values of a feature.

---

[1] As John McCarthy has pointed out, the fact that crosslinguistically high vowels are much more prone to undergo rounding harmony than nonhigh vowels might be attributed to a combination of articulatory and acoustic factors: A distinctive rounding gesture is more difficult to achieve in open vowels, and there is probably a tendency to avoid merging the formants F_1 and F_2, which are already close in low vowels and would get still closer through rounding, which depresses F_2.

1.2.3 Kirghiz dependent rounding harmony

If fusional harmony and spreading harmony both exist, with separate empirical domains, we might expect to find languages where they coexist, leading to a surface harmony pattern which can be viewed as resulting from the union of fusion and spreading. A case of this kind is found in the Altaic language Kirghiz, and I will show in this section that dependent tier ordering can shed light on the interesting harmony phenomena encountered in this language (Johnson 1980, Steriade ms.).

The vowel inventory of Kirghiz is identical to that of Turkish, and we find both backness harmony and rounding harmony. Kirghiz rounding harmony differs from Turkish rounding harmony in interesting ways. Consider the harmonic behavior of the past participle suffix -gAn and the definite past suffix -dI illustrated in (14) (where A and I stand for vocalic archisegments solely specified for height; a rule of voicing assimilation applies to the suffix-initial consonants).

(14)   -gAn   -dI

Past Part. Def. Past

          bil-gen   bil-di   'know'
          ber-gen   ber-di   'give'
          kül-gön   kül-dü   'laugh'
          kör-gön   kör-dü   'see'

          kɨl-gan   kɨl-dɨ   'do, perform'
          al-gan   al-dɨ   'take'
          tut-kan   tut-tu   'hold'
          bol-gon   bol-du   'be, become'

The rounding harmony pattern of Kirghiz becomes clearer when presented in matrix form, as in (15).

(15)

V_1 \ V_2	I	A
u	u u	$\boxed{\text{u a}}$
ü	ü ü	ü ö
o	o u	o o
ö	ö ü	ö ö

Let us examine this pattern in detail. Rounding is transmitted between vowels of like height (kül-dI → kül-dü, tut-dI → tut-tu; kör-gAn → kör-gön, bol-gAn → bolgon). Rounding is also transmitted from non-high vowels to high vowels (kör-dI → kör-dü, bol-dI → bol-du). The one situation where rounding harmony fails is from high vowels to non-high vowels (tut-gAn → tut-kan, *tut-kon). But there is an exception to this exception:

a front rounded high vowel (ü) does transmit rounding to a following non-high vowel (kül-gAn -> kül-gön). This difference in harmonic potential between <u>front</u> rounded high vowels and <u>back</u> rounded high vowels is entirely systematic, as shown in (16) for two other suffixes with low vowels.

(16)
    körün-öt 'appears'   vs.   oltur-at 'is sitting'
    üy-dön 'house-ABL' vs.   turmuš-tan 'lake-ABL'

Instead of positing a single harmony rule[2], we will view the Kirghiz rounding harmony effects as being due

---

[2]Johnson (1980, 91) formulates the following harmony rule:

(i)

$$V \rightarrow [+round] / \begin{bmatrix} V \\ a\ hi \\ b\ bk \\ +\ rd \end{bmatrix} C_0 \begin{bmatrix} \\ g\ hi \end{bmatrix}$$

Condition: $(a, b, g) \neq (+, +, -)$

It is irrelevant in the present context that the rule is stated in segmental terms. The important point is that rounding disharmony is seen as a characteristic of an essentially arbitrary constellation of feature coefficients.

to several sources. We can, as it were, understand Kirghiz rounding harmony as a superposition of three elementary rounding harmony processes: (i) Spreading of [+round] to high vowels, as in Turkish, (ii) height-stratified transmission of [+round], as in Yokuts, and (iii) dependent spreading harmony, to which we turn below. The coexistence of spreading harmony and fusional harmony illustrates the independence of these two mechanisms.

First, there is a rule spreading [+round] onto high vowels. This is a familiar process and constitutes the only kind of rounding harmony to be found in Turkish, as discussed in the preceding section.

Assuming that [round] and [high] are represented on separate tiers and leaving the position of the backness tier for the moment undetermined, we can formulate the rule as in (17).

(17)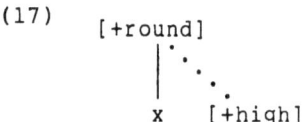

This rule applies in the example /bol-dI/ → <u>bol-du</u> as illustrated in (18).

(18)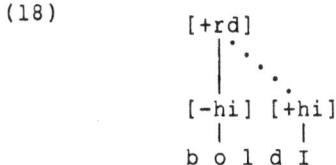
           [+rd]
           |⋱
           | ⋱
           [-hi] [+hi]
            | |
            b o l d I

Secondly, we find in Kirghiz the height-stratified transmission of rounding encountered in Yawelmani Yokuts. This, as we have seen above, does not involve a spreading rule at all, but is a consequence of fusional tier conflation applying to a dependency system of tiers. As shown in (19), fusional tier conflation converts /bol+gAn/ and /tut+dI/ into <u>bolgon</u> and <u>tuttu</u>, respectively.

(19)
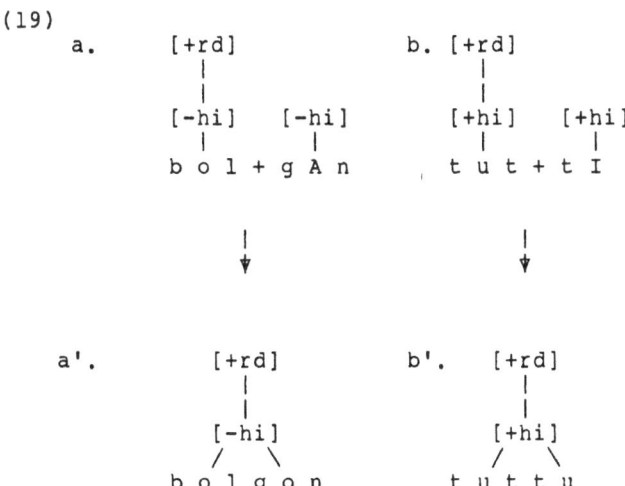

We must now ask how backness harmony fits into this picture, and we also have to account for the remaining cases of rounding harmony, where front (in contrast to back) rounded high vowels affect following nonhigh vowels (/kül+gAn/ -> külgön). As it turns out, these questions are closely related. Building on an idea in Steriade (ms.)[3], we can explain the puzzling rounding effect in forms like külgön if we conceive of backness harmony in terms of underspecification. Let us assume that only [-back] is specified in underlying representations and is the only feature value which is spread by backness harmony, whereas [+back] is just filled in by later default rules. Coupling this assumption with a tier ordering in which [round] is dependent on [back], the rounding effect in külgön is seen to be another consequence of dependent tier ordering. The harmonic transmission of the feature [+round] is parasitic on 'active' backness harmony, which only applies to [-back].

---

[3]Steriade (ms.) combines the theory of underspecification with a revised form of the metrical theory of harmony developed in Halle and Vergnaud (1980).

Consider the representations in (20).

(20) a.
```
        [+rd]
         |
        [-bk]
        |⋱
        |  ⋱
      [+hi] [-hi]
        |     |
      k ü l g A n
```
       külgon

b.
```
        [-bk]
        |⋱
        |  ⋱
      [+hi] [-hi]
        |     |
      b i l g A n
```
       bilgen

In (20) [-back] spreads by Backness Harmony. Because the [round] tier is dependent on the [back] tier in (20a), this automatically also establishes a connection between the [+round] autosegment and the second vowel. In (20b), [-round] is supplied by default. Kirghiz ostensibly has no spreading of [+round] from high vowels onto nonhigh vowels, otherwise we would expect *tut-kon instead of tut-kan. Thus, the rounding influence exerted from front rounded vowels is an automatic consequence of backness harmony and tier structure.

An interesting problem arises when the stem vowel is [-back] and unspecified for rounding but the suffix vowel is lexically specified as [+round] (e.g. -OO nominalizing suffix, /bir+OO/ --> biröö 'the one'. The effect of such backness spreading is shown in (21).

(21)

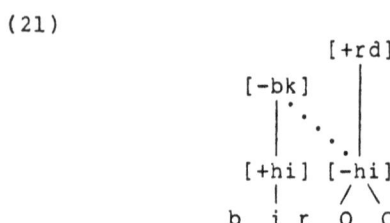

The structure in (21) makes it clear why the [+round] feature of the suffix does not act parasitically: It is not dependent on the [-back] feature which spreads.[4]

---

[4]Structures such as (21) are misaligned as a result of the application of a phonological (spreading) rule. Along lines suggested to me by Alan Prince, I will assume that, as part of Tier Conflation, Tier Alignment takes place which reorganizes misaligned tier structures. Thus the structure in (21) realigns as (i), where the features [+round] and [-back] occupy the same matrix, circumventing an OCP violation.

(i)

$$\begin{array}{cc} & \begin{bmatrix} +rd \\ -bk \end{bmatrix} \\ [-bk] & | \\ | & | \\ [+hi] & [-hi] \\ | & /\ \\ b\ \ i\ \ r & o\ \ o \end{array}$$

This realigned structure accounts for two facts. First, the default [-round] can now be assigned solely to the stem vowel i, note that this was impossible in the structure (21). Secondly, it accounts for the further spreading of the suffix vowel features [-back] and [+round] to other suffixes (/bir+OO+nIn/ --> biröönün 'the one's').

To summarize, Kirghiz vowel harmony is a result of the interaction of fusional and spreading harmony. The complex overall harmony pattern is accounted for by the simple interplay of roundness spreading, height fusion, backness spreading, and the dependently ordered tier structure of Kirghiz.

CHAPTER II

THE CONSONANTISM OF JAVANESE MORPHEMES:

A CASE STUDY

2.0 Introduction

In this chapter, the theory of tier structure developed in the preceding chapter will be applied to the extensive system of consonant cooccurrence restrictions governing morphemes in the Western Austronesian language Javanese. The Javanese constraints, whose discovery is due to Uhlenbeck (1949; Uhlenbeck 1950 is a short summary in English), exhibit a striking resemblance to the well-known root structure constraints found in Semitic languages. The latter were first documented and analyzed in Greenberg (1960), where it is shown that Semitic roots are subject to a number of homorganicity constraints which impose severe limits on consonant combinatorics. McCarthy (1985) extended the work of Greenberg (1960) and showed that the root constraints can be understood as OCP-consequences of an articulated tier structure. For example, the consonantal melody of a Semitic root cannot contain combinations of labial consonants like *bb, *bm, *fb, *mf, etc. The exclusion of *bb is a straightforward consequence of the OCP as applied to whole melody elements, and McCarthy (1985) argues that the feature-sized OCP effect excluding all combinations of labial consonants can be understood in terms of a differentiated tier structure in which the primary articulator feature [labial] occupies a tier all by itself and is therefore exposed to the OCP. Similar exclusion phenomena are observed for other homorganic classes of consonants in Semitic root structure.

Root constraints of this kind are obviously not a universal phenomenon, and the Semitic constraints are sometimes viewed as being inextricably linked to the root-and-pattern morphology of Semitic languages, where the consonantal melody of a root is demonstrably independent both of the skeletal templates characterizing the different binyanim and of the vocalic melodies expressing aspect and voice distinctions. It is therefore a significant finding that pervasive homorganicity constraints are not restricted to languages with root-and-pattern morphology. Uhlenbeck (1949), a work which actually predates Greenberg's investigations by a number of years, documents the existence of a very similar system of root constraints in the Western Austronesian language Javanese. For Javanese there is no sense in which consonantal and vocalic melodies are abstracted from verbal forms as autonomous morphological entities. Nevertheless, the consonantal elements of root morphemes are governed by homorganicity constraints closely paralleling those of Semitic in nature and extent. For example, the consonantal melody of a (native) Javanese morpheme does not contain more than one labial element, i.e. *bb, *pp, *mm, *bp, *pb, *bm, *mb, *pm, *mp are all illicit combinations.

Comparing the Javanese constraints with the Semitic root constraints as discussed in McCarthy (1985), we will find that the facts are essentially parallel, modulo differences in the underlying phonological inventories. Thus Semitic languages do not possess, like Javanese, a full system of palatal consonants which act as a class for the OCP. On the other hand, a specific characteristic of the Semitic language family is the existence of a rich system of 'guttural' consonants, and the cooccurrence restrictions into which these consonants enter in Semitic find no counterpart in Javanese. Labials, coronals and velars are barred from cooccurring in both Semitic and Javanese. The similarity between the Semitic and the Javanese constraints argues strongly that we are dealing here with manifestations of universal aspects of tier structure.

With McCarthy (1985), I assume that differentiated melodic tier structure, the OCP and the directionality parameter of association and spreading (left-to-right for Arabic and right-to-left for Javanese) are the theoretical tools by which the cooccurrence restrictions can be

understood. I depart, however, from the assumptions of
McCarthy (1985) in one crucial respect, namely in the scope
of dependent tier ordering versus branching prohibitions
(see section 2.5).

I will show in this chapter that the Javanese root
structure constraints are consequences of the OCP, given
a particular tier geometry. It will be concluded that
the tier structure for Javanese consonants is the one
diagrammed below.

Tier Structure for Javanese Consonants

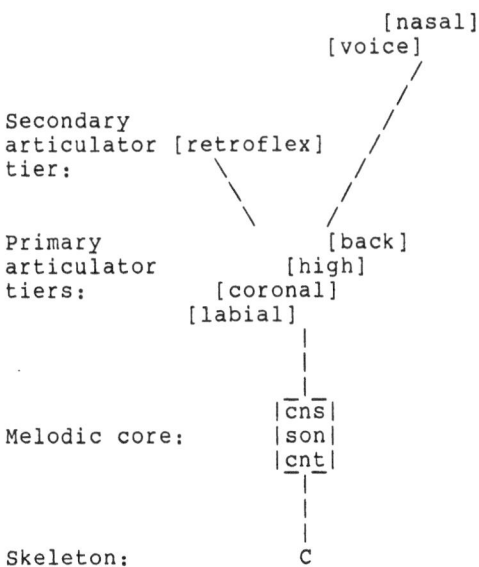

Let me briefly comment on the assumptions underlying this structure.

Besides a basic tier separation between consonantal and vocalic melodies, it is assumed, following McCarthy (1985), that the primary articulator features for consonants ([labial], [coronal], [high], and [back]) each occupy a separate tier. As in Semitic, this separation of articulator tiers explains the existence of nonlocal OCP effects between consonants which are not adjacent on the consonantal tier, i.e. the fact that *ptp is disallowed alongside *pp, in spite of the intervening coronal. Intuitively, what we need is a representation like (i), where the place tier is split into subtiers on one of which the two p's are adjacent; a non-differentiated place tier as in (ii) does not fulfill this requirement.

i.
```
  _____
  ____t_____   coronal tier
  _____
  ___p___p_____   labial tier
```

ii.
```
  _____
  ___p_t_p_____   place tier
```

Voicing, nasality, and retroflexion as a secondary articulation are dependent on the primary articulator features, which in turn are linked to the melodic core units.[1]

Once tiers are differentiated to this degree, with all primary articulator features occupying separate tiers, the core units take on the additional task of ordering the melody elements with respect to each other. We will see below that the sequential order among tautomorphemic consonants must be established independent of the skeleton in order to capture the Javanese consonantal root constraints.

---

[1] There are two special dependencies which are not indicated in (1): The palatal affricates c and j are characterized by a continuancy contour carried by the feature [high] (see section 2.3.2 for discussion), and the glide w is represented with [back] dependent on the primary articulator feature [labial].

2.1. The Javanese Root Constraints:
-the empirical basis-

Let us now investigate the consequences of the OCP for the tier structure given above (p. 89). We will see that to a large extent the cooccurrence restrictions governing Javanese morphemes are automatic consequences of the feature geometry of the consonants.

Javanese Consonant System

LAB	DENT	RETR	PAL	VEL	GLOT
p	t	T	c	k	ʔ
b	d	D	j	g	
			s		h
m	n		ñ	ŋ	
		l			
		r			
w			y		

The segments which appear as retroflex are often classified as alveolars. The fricative s has various phonetic realizations, palatal is only one of them. Morphophonemically it patterns as a palatal in the process of Nasal Substitution (see section 2.3.2). According to Uhrbach (1984), the voiced obstruents are more exactly characterized by breathy voice and impose a distinct breathiness on the following vowel.

Javanese root morphemes are generally built on a bisyllabic template and have the canonical form CVCVC. Roots of other shapes do exist but are far less frequent. Uhlenbeck (1949) examined all morphemes of the form CVCVC occurring in a Javanese-Dutch dictionary and tabulated the phoneme cooccurrences. The data base consists of more than 6000 forms including not only native Javanese morphemes but also many loans from Sanskrit, Arabic, and in particular from Dutch. The data was thus not presifted so as to include only native roots. The fact that nevertheless clear generalizations emerge which are on the whole rather similar to the Semitic root constraints is surprising not only because Javanese is typologically very different from Semitic and has no root-and-pattern morphology with consonantal roots, but also because the data base includes a large number of loans which violate the cooccurrence restrictions holding in the native vocabulary. One consequence of Uhlenbeck's inclusion of loans is that we are in general faced with statistical generalizations which hold for a vast number of morphemes, but which are not exceptionless.

Table I (on the next page) shows the cooccurrence frequencies for all pairs of consonants in positions C_1 and C_2 of $C_1VC_2VC_3$ morphemes.

Table I Javanese C1/C2 Occurrences

C1\C2	p	b	m	w	t	d	T	D	r	l	n	ŋ	s	c	j	y	k	g	ɖ	h	S
p	41	1	9	8	39	7	49	21	64	75	24	4	41	43	17	19	46	26	24	8	566
b	6	45	0	22	28	8	19	48	60	74	24	6	32	21	27	23	29	20	32	4	528
m	4	9	18	15	11	21	16	13	39	44	26	25	19	7	19	20	10	30	23	8	377
w	2	1	0	23	18	18	2	19	31	43	14	1	10	2	22	13	10	9	6	0	244
t	38	29	21	24	46	3	0	15	50	63	19	0	10	0	9	17	40	27	18	5	434
d	3	10	22	7	1	17	0	0	14	39	7	1	3	0	0	5	12	7	3	1	152
T	0	0	7	5	0	0	10	0	8	8	2	0	1	0	0	5	9	0	11	0	66
D	14	5	13	20	3	0	1	32	7	10	5	1	11	5	1	13	29	9	12	9	200
r	28	29	30	37	15	5	0	3	16	4	6	8	20	16	30	35	17	36	18	3	356
l	22	27	42	49	21	13	16	23	68	35	15	14	26	16	17	34	28	30	28	11	535
n	3	1	4	0	5	1	0	1	1	1	13	0	5	2	5	3	7	2	2	4	60
ŋ	1	2	8	0	1	0	3	1	4	0	2	9	0	0	0	1	0	3	4	0	39
s	35	34	38	52	26	11	17	33	76	76	24	0	43	1	8	27	39	30	43	7	620
c	31	21	25	39	7	1	30	15	42	40	11	0	0	43	2	7	54	17	35	2	422
j	10	39	22	26	12	11	7	27	36	29	17	0	3	1	20	6	12	28	10	1	317
y	0	0	0	0	3	0	0	0	0	0	0	0	0	0	0	3	2	1	0	0	9
k	64	37	32	55	55	34	54	32	83	96	39	29	46	50	23	37	46	7	8	3	830
g	23	44	23	25	30	15	38	37	64	59	20	11	27	23	22	22	1	42	0	1	527
ɖ	1	5	1	5	2	2	4	0	9	3	7	6	3	7	2	5	8	1	3	1	73
S	326	339	315	412	323	167	266	320	672	699	275	115	300	235	224	295	399	325	280	68	6355

Table I was established on the basis of Uhlenbeck's overall count (1949: 112-3). C_1 is given vertically, C_2 horizontally. Note that h does not occur initially.

The absolute cooccurrence frequencies given in Table I are difficult to interpret and require some statistical analysis, but they already indicate that there are strong constraints governing the choice of C_1 and C_2. Uhlenbeck (1949) etablished the main generalization: Homorganic consonants exclude each other unless they are identical in all features. Thus among the labial consonants we find that the identity combination p-p occurs in 41 forms, but p-b only once and p-m only 9 times. Similarly b-b occurs in 45 forms, but b-p only 6 times, and b-m not at all. The same basic pattern recurs in other sections of the table. Among the coronal obstruents, the combination t-t appears in 46 morphemes, but t-T not at all, t-d occurs in 3 forms and t-D in 15; d-d occurs in 17 forms, d-t once, and d-T and d-D are not found at all. Among the palatal consonants, ñ-ñ appears in 9 morphemes, but ñ-s, ñ-c, and ñ-j are not attested; s-s occurs in 43 morphemes, s-ñ in 0, s-c in 1, s-j in 8 forms, etc.

Such differences in absolute cooccurrence frequencies are instructive, but they cannot form the basis for valid generalizations. The data must be subjected to a statistical analysis which, for each combination of phonemes, weighs the actual number of cooccurrences against the expected number of cooccurrences. It is not enough to know, for example, that p-b occurs less frequently than p-p. What we need to know is whether p-b occurs significantly less frequently than expected, where the expected frequency for p-b is based on the overall frequency of p as C_1 and of b as C_2. If b is quite generally rare in position C_2, irrespective of the nature of the C_1 consonant, it is not surprising that it does not occur very often with initial p, no special dissimilatory relation between p and b can be inferred.

I have used a standard significance test (the chi square test) to determine those combinations of phonemes whose cooccurrence is significantly restricted (with respect to their expected cooccurrence frequency). The exact results are presented in an appendix to this chapter.

If we check the cooccurrence data in Table I for pairs of phonemes which cooccur with significantly low frequency, we obtain Table II (on the next page) as a result. Pairs of phonemes whose actual cooccurrence frequency lies significantly below their expected cooccurrence frequency (level of significance $p < 0.05$, which corresponds to a chi square value > 3.84 on one degree of freedom) are marked by "X" in the appropriate cell.

Table II   Javanese C1/C2   X : Significantly infrequent combination

C1\C2	p	b	m	w	t	d	T	D	r	l	n	s	c	j	y	k	g	ŋ	h
p	X	X																	
b	X	X																	
m	X	X	X													X			
w	X	X	X	X			X												
t						X	X												
d					X	X	X					X	X	X					
T																			
D					X	X	X					X	X	X					
r							X	X	X		X								
l									X	X	X								
n																			
s											X	X	X	X	X				
c						X					X	X	X	X	X				
j						X					X	X	X	X	X				
y																			
k																X	X	X	
g																	X	X	
ŋ																			X

97

An inspection of Table II makes it very clear that the phoneme pairs whose cooccurrence frequency is significantly low are clustering in an area of homorganicity centered around, but not including, the diagonal (strictly speaking, the diagonal of the submatrix not containing h, which does not occur initially). As indicated in Table II, we find systematic exclusion groups: Labial consonants exclude other labials, as do coronal obstruents, coronal sonorants, palatal consonants, and velar consonants. There are some gaps in these patterns, and there is also one asymmetric constraint against coronal consonants in Cl combined with palatal consonants in C_2. Abstracting away from these complications, we find an overall homorganic exclusion system as indicated in Table III.

Table III

C1\ \C2	Labials	Coronal Obstruents	Coronal Sonorants	Palatals	Velars
Labials	✕				
Coronal Obstruents		✕			
Coronal Sonorants			✕		
Palatals				✕	
Velars					✕

2.2 Directional Association and Spreading

In Table III we have neglected the fact that identical consonants can in general cooccur in C_1/C_2, in apparent violation of the homorganicity constraint. The diagonal of Table II shows no entries,[1] whereas the cooccurrence of homorganic but nonidentical consonants is severely restricted. This is reminiscent of the distribution of consonants in Semitic verbal forms, where C_2 and C_3 in forms of the shape $C_1VC_2VC_3$ can be identical (e.g. samam 'to poison') but cannot be homorganic if nonidentical (there are no forms like *sabam). McCarthy (1979, 1981) explained forms like samam as involving a biconsonantal root melody sm which is associated (left-to-right) with a CVCVC template; the second root consonant then spreads to the unfilled template-final C slot. The left-to-right directionality of association and spreading also explains the fact that identity of C_1 and C_2 is not allowed in Semitic. The Javanese facts suggest a similar analysis, but with the opposite direction of association and spreading, namely right-to-left instead of left-to-right. Take an example like babot 'carpet'. Suppose this forms consists of a template CVCVC, a consonantal melody bt and

---

[1] On the two apparent exceptions among the liquids see section 2.5 and section 2.7.6 of the appendix.

a vocalic melody <u>ao</u>. The melodies are associated right-to-left with the template, deriving (1a). Subsequent right-to-left melody spread to unfilled skeletal positions derives (1b).

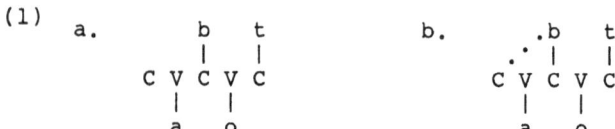

Spreading of a whole melody element amounts to spreading of its melodic core, and the representation of <u>babot</u> after right-to-left association and spreading is more exactly the one given in (2).

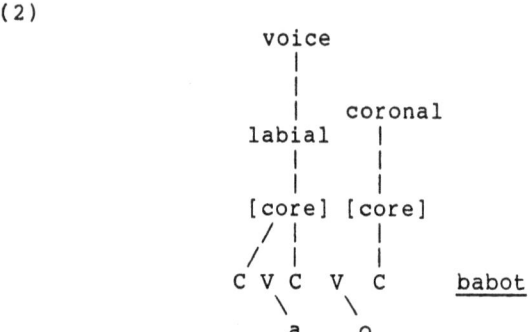

If we interpret the identity cases in this way as involving the spreading of a whole melody element, we obtain for the underlying consonantal melodies of roots the generalization that all homorganic combinations are excluded. Thus surface sequences of the form b_V_b_, p_V_p_, m_V_m_ etc. within morphemes are not represented as sequences of melody elements but rather as single melody elements associated with two skeleton positions.

This account for cooccurrences of identical consonants makes a clear prediction: Given the right-to-left direction of association and spreading in Javanese, multiple linking between melodic core and skeleton should be restricted to the left edges of morphemes and not occur in C_2/C_3. This prediction is in fact borne out.[2] Uhlenbeck (1949, 124) characterizes the basic difference between C_1/C_2 and C_2/C_3 combinations as follows:

> Terwijl gelijkheid tussen de 1ste en de 2de consonant vaak voorkomt en blijkbaar een geliefde combinatie vormt, blijkt ten aanzien van de 2de en 3de consonant juist het tegendeel. Er is juist en afkeer van gelijkheid [...].
>
> ["While identity of the first and second consonant occurs frequently and apparently constitutes a popular combination, just the opposite appears to hold for the second and third consonant. There is precisely an aversion against identity."]

---

[2] The situation is somewhat complicated by the fact that a number of contrasts are neutralized in the final C_3 position, see section 2.1.3.

For example, while morphemes of the form papat are frequent, forms like *tapap are hardly attested. Uhlenbeck (1949, 125-6) shows that the existing cases of this kind are mostly of a special character and involve loanwords, obscured morpheme combinations or expressive morphemes.

This asymmetry in the distribution of identical consonant combinations in Javanese, the mirror image of the Semitic pattern, follows from right-to-left association and spreading:

(3)

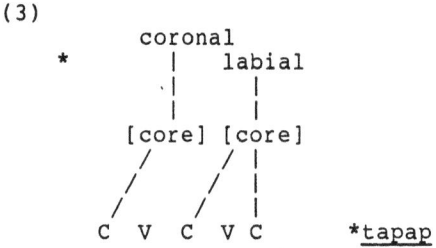

In the structure (3), the spreading option is utilized before the one-to-one association of melody units and skeletal units from right-to-left is completed.

2.3 OCP-interactions of Primary Articulator Features

We have seen that surface combinations of identical consonants do not constitute sequences of melody elements, but are properly analyzed as single melody elements linked to two skeleton positions.

I will now show that the incompatibility of nonidentical homorganics follows from the structure of the Javanese tier system. The basic idea is that dependent tier ordering leads to OCP violations in all such cases.

2.3.1 Nasality and Voicing as Dependent Tiers

Let us begin by considering the dependently ordered voicing and nasal tiers. It is not possible to represent two homorganic consonants differing in voicing or nasality within the same morpheme without violating the OCP. Consider for example the labial combinations in (1). In order to simplify the representations, I will from now on use the alphabetic symbol corresponding to a segment as an abbreviation for its melodic core and the features contained in it whenever the core specifications are not themselves at issue.

(1)

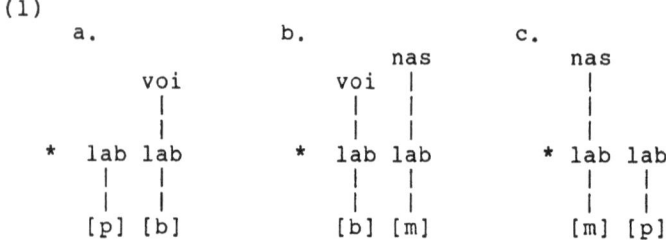

Since the voicing and nasal tiers have direct access only to the place tiers, two separate labial autosegments are necessary to carry the voicing and nasal specifications for the two consonants in these forms, in violation of the OCP.[1] Combinations of different primary articulators are no problem, because either one of them can carry the nasal or voicing feature alone, as in (2), or share it with the other primary articulator, as in (3).

(2)

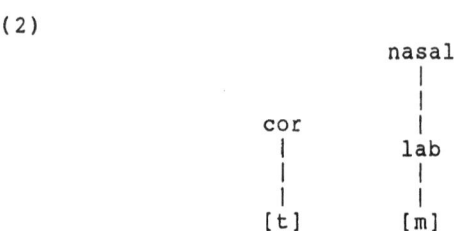

---

[1] A dependency explanation of this kind for the Javanese root constraints has been independently suggested in Kenstowicz (1986).

(3)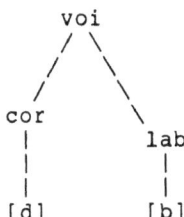

For the labial and velar consonants the position of voicing and nasality in Javanese tier structure is sufficient to derive the incompatibility of homorganics. In order to explain the fact that the labial glide w shows significant OCP-interactions with the other labials, I assume that w is represented with [back] as a secondary articulation dependent on [labial] and is therefore incompatible with p, b, and m.

2.3.2   Palatals : Continuancy as a Dependent Tier

Palatals are characterized by the primary articulator feature [high]. Besides the dependent tiers for voicing and nasal, there is another dependent tier which is exclusively defined on the [high] tier, namely the continuancy contour for the palatal affricates. The palatal consonants of Javanese have the following structures:

(4)

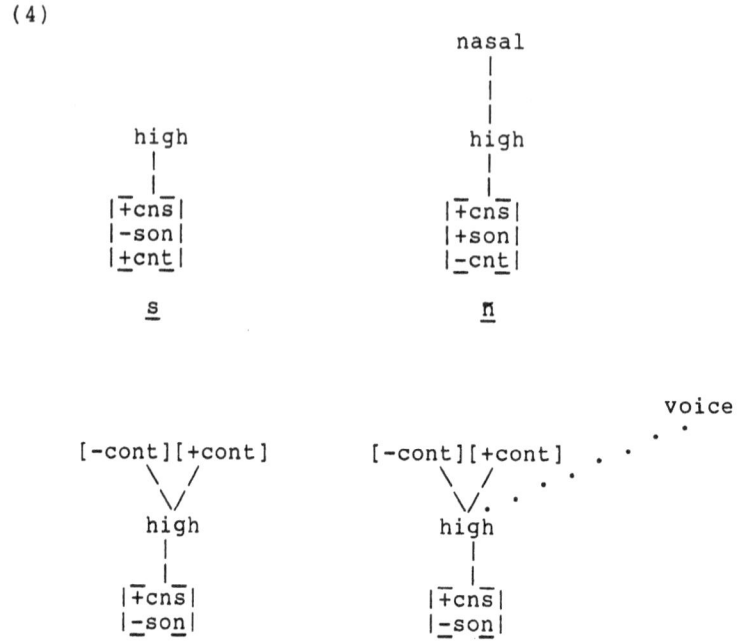

While the nonaffricates s̱ and ṉ have their continuancy specification in the melodic core, the affricates c̱ and ȷ̱ are represented as single melody elements, with the place feature [high] carrying a dependent continuancy contour. In representing affricates as single melody elements with an internal branching structure and not as sequences of melody elements linked to a single skeletal C, as was proposed in Clements and Keyser (1983), I follow a recent suggestion by McCarthy and Prince (in preparation). The authors note that a structure with internal branching explains why affricates always share some features and correctly predicts that they behave as single units with respect to metathesis rules and under association in reduplicative and root-and-pattern systems.

The inclusion of s̲ among the palatals merits some discussion. Like many Austronesian languages, Javanese has only a single oral fricative s̲. According to Uhlenbeck (1949, 54), Javanese s̲ has both dental and palatal realizations. With respect to the cooccurrence restrictions, s̲ clearly behaves as an underlying palatal (see the cooccurrence data in section 2.7.2 of the appendix). As also pointed out by Uhlenbeck (1949, 54), this finds independent support in the morphophonemic behavior of s̲. The crucial evidence appears in the lexical process of Nasal Substitution, which derives active forms of verbs from roots. We cannot enter here into the details of a full analysis of Nasal Substitution, in the present context it is sufficient to note that root-initial voiceless obstruents are replaced by their homorganic nasals.[2] The pattern is shown in (5).

---

[2]The retroflex stop T is replaced by n̲, which can be attributed to structure preservation: Since there is no underlying retroflex nasal N̲, the lexical process of Nasal Substitution cannot create such a segment, and the lexical default nasal n̲ appears instead.

(5)

	ROOT	ACTIVE FORM	
p->m	paɲan	maɲan	'eat'
t->n	tug@l	nug@l	'break in two'
T->n	Tukol	nukol	'grow'
c->ɲ	c@Da?	ɲ@Da?	'approach'
k->ŋ	k@r@t	ŋ@r@t	'cut'

(The symbol @ stands for schwa.)

The underlying palatal nature of s manifests itself in the fact that it is replaced by the palatal nasal ɲ in Nasal Substitution, as illustrated by the following examples in (6).

(6)

ROOT	ACTIVE FORM	
saged	ɲaged	'be able'
seDeŋ	ɲeDeŋ	'last, fit'
sinau	ɲinau	'learn'
sowan	ɲowan	'visit'
surat	ɲurat	'write'

Returning to the feature structures given above in (4), we see that all combinations of palatals would involve an illicit sequence of the form "[high] [high]" and are therefore ruled out. In particular, the dependent position of the continuancy contour makes cooccurrences of c and s impossible, as shown in (7).

(7)
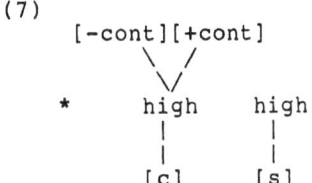

2.3.3   Coronals and Retroflexion

Let us now consider the OCP-interactions which involve the feature [coronal]. An interesting property of the homorganicity constraints in Javanese (which is also observed in Semitic) is the fact that the coronal sonorants l, r, and n show no tendency towards OCP-interaction with the coronal obstruents but rather act as if they constitute an entirely separate category. Consider the Javanese system of coronals given in (8) (where T and D are retroflex stops):

(8)
```
            t    T
            d    D
            ------
            n
            ------
                 l
                 r
```

The coronal obstruents $\underline{t}$, $\underline{d}$, $\underline{T}$, and $\underline{D}$ show significant OCP-interactions among themselves, but do not interact with the nasal $\underline{n}$ or with the liquids $\underline{l}$ and $\underline{r}$. For example, in Table I (section 2.1) we find the following cooccurrence frequencies: t_1/n_2 19, t_1/l_2 63, t_1/r_2 50, d_1/n_2 7, d_1/l_2 39, d_1/r_2 14. When weighed against the expected cooccurrence frequencies (which is important, because initial $\underline{d}$ is far less frequent than initial $\underline{t}$), none of these numbers is significantly low.[3]

As we will see below, there are also OCP-interactions inside the system of coronal sonorants. While $\underline{r}$ and $\underline{l}$ cooccur quite freely with $\underline{n}$, the cooccurrence patterns of liquids are highly restricted.

Thus each of the sets {t, d, T, D}, {n}, {l, r} constitutes an exclusion system of its own, and elements from different sets can be quite freely combined. It is important to bear in mind that this is a fact about <u>coronal</u> sonorants and not about sonorants in general. The labial nasal $\underline{m}$ shows quite pronounced OCP-interactions with homorganic obstruents, and the same holds for the palatal nasal $\underline{ñ}$ and the velar nasal $\underline{ŋ}$.

---

[3] There is one systematic prohibition against the cooccurrence of $\underline{T}$, $\underline{D}$ with $\underline{r}$, explicable as an OCP-interaction involving the feature [retroflex]. We will ignore this interaction for the time being and return to it in section 2.5.

A natural way of explaining the combinability of coronal sonorants with coronal obstruents is to appeal to underspecification. Let us hypothesize that the dental nasal n̪ and the liquids are not specified for coronality in the lexicon, but acquire this feature by later default rules. Obstruents, on the other hand, are fully specified for coronality. This assumption then explains why there are no OCP-interactions between coronal sonorants and coronal obstruents. The compatibility of coronal obstruents with coronal sonorants is not specific to Javanese, but is also observed in Semitic (Greenberg 1960, McCarthy 1985), and the appeal to underspecification has the virtue of providing a general answer to this kind of combinability. I will assume the following representations for Javanese coronals.

(9)
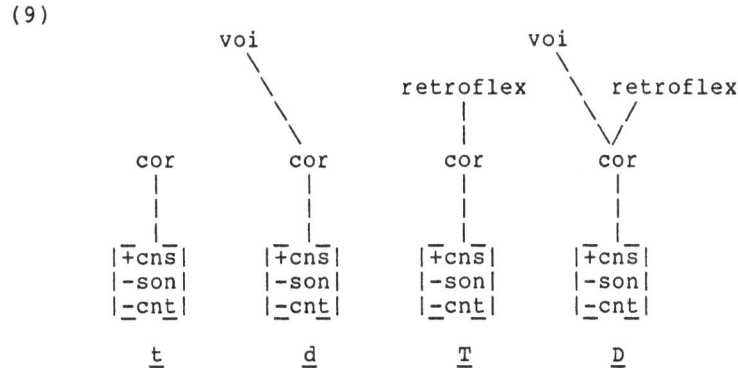

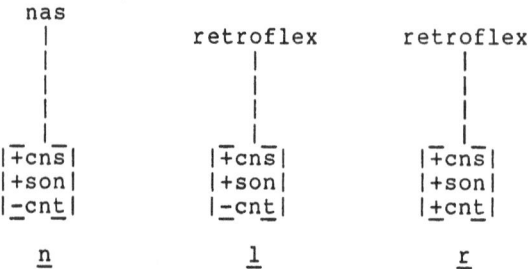

The feature [retroflex], as a secondary articulation, is mapped into the place feature [coronal] for the retroflex stops T and D. In the case of the sonorants, however, the features [nasal] and [retroflex], in the absence of a place feature they could attach to, are directly linked to the core. The liquids l and r are differentiated by different values for continuancy. Both are specified as retroflex.

Given these feature structures for the coronal segments, in particular given the underspecification of sonorants for coronality, the OCP rules out cooccurrences of coronal obstruents, as illustrated in (10a), but no OCP conflict arises between coronal sonorants and coronal obstruents, as shown in (10b).

(10)

Furthermore, the coronal underspecification for [n] captures the difference between the grammatical dn-sequence (11a) versus the ungrammatical *gŋ-sequence (11b).

(11)

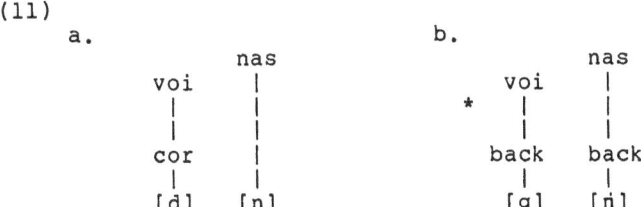

2.3.4   Root-final consonants

The cooccurrence data involving root-final consonants as they appear in Uhlenbeck (1949) are somewhat difficult to interpret since this position in Javanese has special properties and can be occupied only by a limited class of segments. For example, the retroflex obstruents T and D, the palatals c, j, and ñ, and the glides w and y do not occur at the end of morphemes. Further complications result from the fact that Uhlenbeck (1949) based his cooccurrence counts on the isolation forms of morphemes, which show the effects of rules applying to word-final consonants (devoicing of all voiced obstruents and replacement of /k/ by [?] everywhere except after /@/).

In view of this situation it is not too astonishing that the OCP-behavior involving root-final consonants is not entirely clearcut.

However, final consonants in Javanese morphemes are by no means universally immune to the OCP, and there are two classes of segments which show clear OCP-effects, namely labials (discussed immediately below) and liquids (to be discussed in section 2.5).

With some idealisation (cf. section 2.7.5 in the appendix for details) we can state that in Javanese morphemes of the form $C_1VC_2VC_3$, labials do not cooccur either in C_2/C_3 or in C_1/C_3.

What is of interest here is that neither nonidentical labials nor identical labials cooccur in these positions. We expect nonidentical labials to be ruled out by the OCP on the labial tier (see section 2.3.1 above and related discussion). However, the restriction on identical labials in these positions cannot be attributed to the OCP, because they can in principle be represented as multiply linked single melody elements. As was already pointed out in section 2.2, the asymmetry between allowed identity in C_1/C_2 and the exclusion of identity in C_2/C_3 follows from right-to-left association of melody to skeleton in Javanese: The structure in (12a) but not the structure in (12b) is produced by right-to-left mapping.

(12)

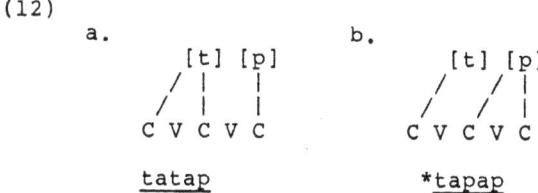

We might consider representing *tapap with a single [labial] feature linked to two identical melodic cores, as in (13). This circumvents the association problem (note the one-to-one mapping from melodic core to skeleton) but violates the Geminate Minimization Principle (repeated in (14)).

(13)

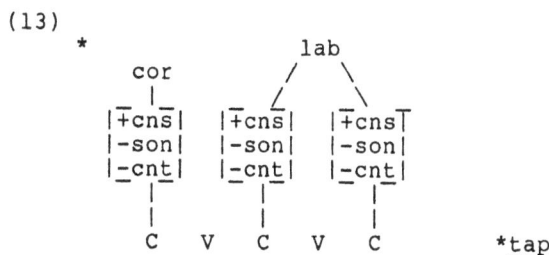

(14)
Geminate Minimization Principle

Melodic structures of the form (i) are illformed, where [core$_x$] and [core$_y$] are identical core configurations sharing all external feature specifications.

(i)
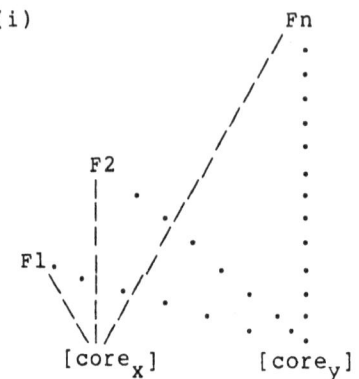

Thus the theoretical apparatus which is independently motivated and the proposed Javanese tier structure predicts correctly that identical labials do not cooccur in C_2/C_3.

Let us then consider the exclusion of identical labials from C_1/C_3. In order to rule out the consonantal sequence *ptp by the OCP, we rely crucially on the assumption that the primary articulator features occupy different tiers:

(15)

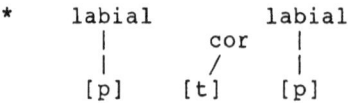

If they were lined up on a single place tier, a structure like (16) would be entirely compatible with the OCP:

(16)
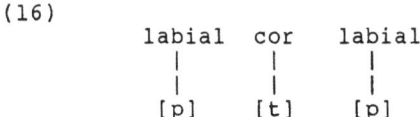

On the other hand, the tier separation of [coronal] and [labial] now apparently allows (17) as another potential structure for *ptp, with [labial] multiply linked to two nonadjacent identical cores. Since the intervening [coronal] occupies a separate tier, there is no crossing of association lines.

(17)
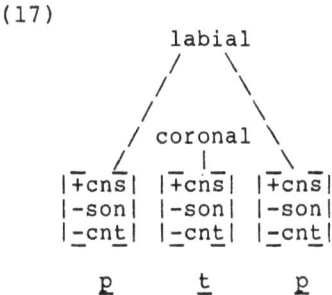

However, we can interpret the Geminate Minimization Principle (14) in such a way that it rules out (17) on a par with (13). Note that (14) does not stipulate that the two core units involved have to be adjacent. Let us adopt the most general interpretation of the Geminate Minimization Principle (14) as a working hypothesis, such that it holds for both adjacent and nonadjacent cores. Under this assumption, the multiple linking of [labial] in (17) is ruled out by (14) without extra stipulations. Note that because of the intervening t̲ a form like *<u>patap</u> cannot result from spreading of the melodic core, as in (18), because this would violate the universal autosegmental prohibition on line-crossing.

(18)
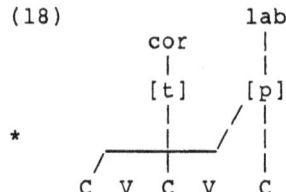

2.4 The Representation of Exceptional Forms

In this section I will discuss the question of how to represent exceptional forms which violate the cooccurrence restrictions holding for the vast majority of the morphemes in the Javanese lexicon. I will use the labials as an example case. As we have seen, the tier geometry which we have assumed for Javanese, together with the OCP, rules out all cooccurrences of labials. This leaves us with the question of how to represent the few exceptional forms showing violations of the labial cooccurrence restriction, as e.g. the Dutch loanword bipet 'buffet'. We cannot very well say that such forms simply violate the OCP, since we are assuming, with McCarthy (1986), that the OCP is a universal constraint and not a principle of markedness. Surface violations of the labial cooccurrence restriction should therefore have a 'marked' tier structure which, while conforming to the OCP, also accounts for their peripheral status in the language.

A reasonable hypothesis for forms like bipet 'buffet' is that they are represented with consonants and vowels occupying the same tier. Such a representation receives independent support from facts about the vocalism of such loanwords. In bisyllabic Javanese morphemes the vocalism of the two syllables is governed by a prohibition against cooccurrences of mid and high vowels (see Uhlenbeck 1949, 97-107). Forms with vowel combinations like i-e, i-o etc. are extremely rare in the native vocabulary. This restriction is however frequently violated in loanwords, for example in the above-mentioned form bipet. Without entering here into a discussion of the phonology of Javanese vowels (see Kenstowicz 1986 for an interesting analysis which strongly argues that the postulation of a vowel tier is necessary for an adequate understanding of Javanese vowel phonology), we can assume that the constraint ruling out sequences like i-e in native morphemes, where vowels and consonants are segregated, is inapplicable in morphemes with consonants and vowels on the same tier. Postulating a uniform melody tier shared by consonants and vowels immmediately leads us to expect double exceptionality in such loans, namely unusual consonant combinations as well as unusual vowel combinations, and this is what we typically find, according to Uhlenbeck (1949, 121).

It is not quite clear whether the assumption of a combined vowel-consonant tier is appropriate for native morphemes with irregular labial combinations. Such forms are exceedingly rare, apparently bapa? 'father, sir' is the only one in common use. According to Dudas (1976, 51-2), there exists a variant pronunciation bapa without final glottal stop. Suppose this form is also represented

with consonants and vowels on the same tier. This would
then predict that the rule in (1), which otherwise applies
across-the-board (ATB) to successive occurrences of a (see
Kenstowicz 1986), as e.g. in (2), should only apply to
the second occurrence of a in bapa.

(1)
$\quad$ a → O / __ #   (O = lax o)

(2)
$\quad\quad\quad$ /kanca/ → kOncO   'friend'
$\quad\quad\quad\quad\quad\;\;$ kanca-ne 'my friend'

But rule (1) appears to apply ATB to both occurrences
of a: bOpO 'father', bapa-ne 'my father'. This would
not be possible under the assumption that the irregular
labial combination forces consonants and vowels on a single
tier in such forms. It is worth pointing out that there
are several unresolved questions concerning rule (1), as
noted in Kenstowicz (1986), in particular the problem that
the ATB application of (1) seems to violate geminate
inalterability. If we disregard this and take the vocalism
of bOpO as evidence that consonantal and vocalic melodies
are segregated in this form, then it must have a special
tier structure in some other way, in order to be compatible
with the OCP. For example, bapa could be exceptional,
as shown in (3), with voicing directly linked to the core

instead of to the place feature and with a doubly linked
[labial] feature.

(3)
```
         [labial]
        /   \    [voice]
       /     \   /
    |+cns|  |+cns|
    |-son|  |-son|
    |-cnt|  |-cnt|
      |       |
      C   V   C   V
           \     /
            \   /
             a         bapa   'father'
```

This might in fact be appropriate, given the isolated
status of this word.

2.5 Branching Prohibitions and Geminate Minimization

In accounting for the cooccurrence restrictions on
homorganics governing Semitic root structure, McCarthy
(1985) utilizes branching prohibitions as the main
analytical tool. For example, the voicing feature is taken
as part of the melodic core, and the incompatibility of
f and b in Arabic roots is explained by appealing to a
constraint prohibiting branching of the feature [labial].
The structure for *fb in (1), while in compliance with

the OCP, is ruled out because it contains a multiply linked
[labial] feature.

(1)
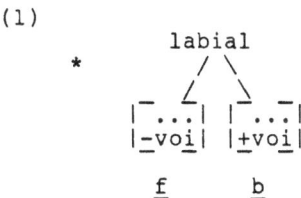

Our explanation for parallel phenomena in Javanese is based on the dependent ordering of the voicing tier on the primary articulators (see section 2.3.1). It is possible to follow this strategy here, too, and to account for the incompatibility of f and b in Arabic without postulating a branching prohibition for [labial]. If voicing is dependent on the primary articulator features, the only representation which expresses the sequence f-b violates the OCP on the [labial] tier, as shown in (2).

(2)
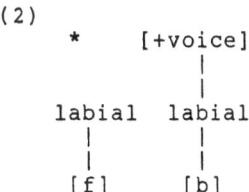

As discussed in Chapter I, although branching prohibitions and dependent ordering often allow alternative analyses in an OCP-based approach, both of these mechanisms constitute independently necessary parts of the theory. The evidence from Ngbaka (see chapter I, section 1.1.3) shows that a certain amount of dependent ordering is necessary. We also find the opposite situation, namely where only a branching prohibition but not dependent ordering can account for the facts. We will encounter such a case from Javanese immediately below, where the cooccurrence restriction governing the secondary feature [retroflex] can only be adequately captured by a branching prohibition.

The cooccurrence restrictions which we have so far considered are all of the symmetric type, that is, the order *pb is ruled out together with the order *bp. An interesting example of an asymmetric restriction is found in the distribution of liquids in Javanese morphemes.[1]

A single liquid in a CVCVC morpheme can occur initially, medially, or finally, without any restrictions, as illustrated in (3).

---

[1] Another asymmetric cooccurrence restriction is found between palatals and coronals and is discussed in the appendix.

(3) a. liw@t   'boil rice'   r@se?   'clean'
         l@pas   'free'   rak@t   'close'

     b. dolan   'amuse o.s.'   turah   'remain'
         g@l@m   'be willing'   b@ras   'uncooked rice'

     c. mucal   'teach'   bakar   'roast'
         bakal   'intend   pasar   'market'

When a morpheme contains more than one liquid, however, the cooccurrence possibilities are highly restricted. The basic generalisations can be formulated as follows (see Uhlenbeck 1949, 128-9 and section 2.7.6 of the appendix to this chapter for an detailed analysis of the cooccurrence data):

(i) The identity combinations ll and rr occur only in C_1/C_2.[2]

(ii) If a morpheme contains two different liquids, the first one must be l.

Schematically, the possibilities for cooccurrences of liquids in $C_1VC_2VC_3$ morphemes are as follows:

---

[2] By a historical process of liquid dissimilation, many of the rr sequences have been changed to lr, and this has led in a number of cases to the existence of doublets like raras ~ laras 'sound, harmony' (see section 2.7.6 of the appendix for further discussion).

(4)
```
C₁/C₂:      lvrVC       lvlVC       rVrVC  | * rVlVC
C₂/C₃:      CVlVr |  * CVlVl    * CVrVr    * CVrVl
C₁/C₃:      lVCVr |  * lVCVl    * rVCVr    * rVCVl
```

In the last section we argued that the coronal sonorants are lexically not specified for coronality, accounting in this way for their compatibility with coronal stops. The segments l and r are both retroflex, they are differentiated by different values for continuancy, as illustrated in (5). I am assuming that l gets specified for laterality by a default rule.

(5)
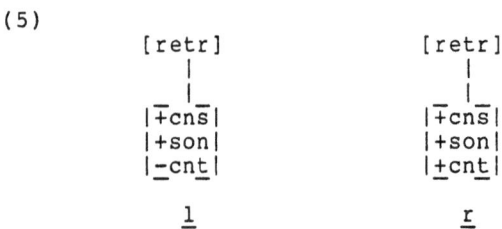

The basic generalization about cooccurrences of liquids is that r cannot precede l, whereas l can precede r. We can capture this asymmetric restriction if we constrain the branching possibilities for the feature [retroflex] in the way indicated in (6).

(6)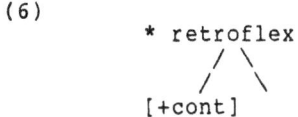

The branching prohibition in (6) rules out all representations in which the first branch of a doubly linked [retroflex] feature is occupied by a [+continuant] segment, i.e. by r. For example, l@r@n 'stop, rest' and tular 'infect' have the wellformed representations (7a,b), whereas hypothetical *r@l@n and *tural in (8a,b) violate the branching constraint (6).

(7)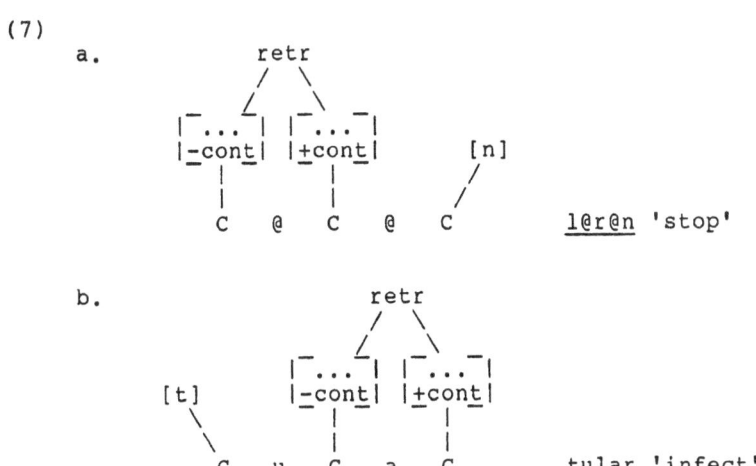

(8) a.

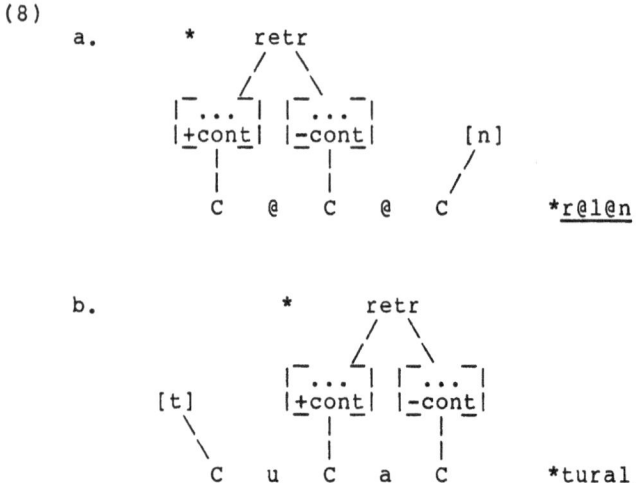

*r@l@n

b.

*tural

In C_1/C_3 the order rl which violates (6) is found in a fair number of loanwords (see section 2.7.6 of the appendix). If we follow Uhlenbeck's (1949, 129) assessment and regard morphemes with initial r and final l as exceptional, we can maintain that (6) also holds in nonadjacency, as illustrated in (9a,b).

(9) a.

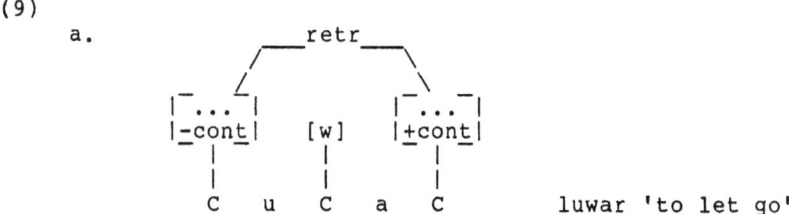

luwar 'to let go'

b. 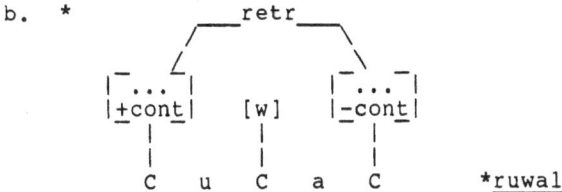   *ruwal

In this way, the directional restriction ruling out the order rl while allowing the order lr follows from (6).

This constraint not only explains the fundamental asymmetry observed in liquid combinations (*rl does not occur but lr is wellformed), but also accounts for the one significant exclusion relation holding between coronal obstruents and coronal sonorants. It is found between the retroflex obstruents T D and the liquid r (see 2.7.7 in the appendix) and concerns the combinations *rT and *rD. This restriction does not involve an extra stiplulation, since it already follows from the retroflexion constraint, which does not allow a representation like (10) while permitting (11).

(10)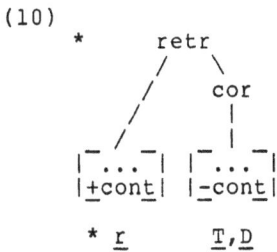

(11)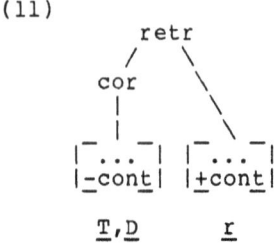

Thus the retroflexion constraint repeated below accounts for the exclusion of the consonantal sequences *rl, *rD and *rT.

(12)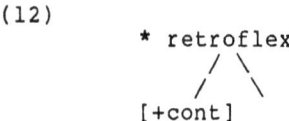

It should be noted that a feature-specific branching prohibition such as (12) is not equivalent to the Geminate Minimization Principle. Consider the structures in (13), both representing leleh 'soft'.

(13)   a.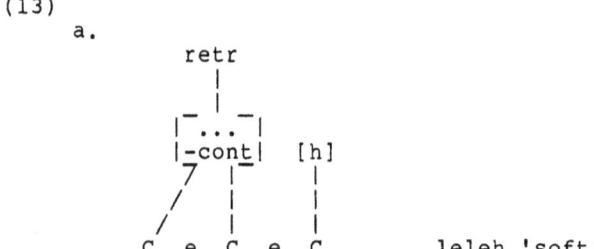

leleh 'soft'

```
    b.          retr
              /   \
             /     \
          _ /_   _ \_
         |...| |...|
         |-cont| |-cont|   [h]
           |     |       |
           |     |       |
           C  e  C  e    C       leleh 'soft'
```

In (13a), a single melodic core is linked to two skeleton positions (by right-to left association and subsequent spreading of the core), and in (13b) a single place feature is linked to two core units which are each separately associated to the skeletal units. Neither the structure in (13a) nor that in (13b) violates the branching prohibition in (12). In the former structure, [retroflex] simply does not branch, and in the latter structure, although retroflex branches, the left branch is not linked to a [+cont] core. As discussed in section 1.1, such representational ambiguities are clearly undesirable and have to be ruled out in principle. The structure in (13b), where the feature [retroflex] branches to identical core configurations, violates the Geminate Minimization Principle which says that identical core units cannot share all melodic features. The principle of Geminate Minimization is therefore independently needed aside from any branching prohibitions that a language may posit.

Thus a theory accounting for cooccurrence restrictions in an OCP-based approach contains dependent ordering possibilities, language-specific branching prohibitions, and the universal principle of Geminate Minimization as crucial ingredients. In an attempt to reduce the amount of redundancy inherent in the theoretical framework, we suggested in section 1.1.3 that melody-internal branching prohibitions are limited to certain areas of tier structure; in particular, we hypothesized that the universal linking of primary articulators to the melodic core cannot be made subject to language-particular branching prohibitions. Under this assumption it is impossible to impose a specific branching prohibition on [labial], and a dependency account as proposed in this chapter remains as the only alternative. Such limitation on the domain of branching prohibitions may be difficult to maintain in the light of further empirical evidence, and the proper division of labor between branching prohibitions and dependent tier ordering is a problem which clearly deserves future exploration.

2.6 Summary and Concluding Remarks

We have seen in this chapter that an articulated tier geometry accounts for the consonant cooccurrence restrictions governing Javanese morphemes. In particular, we have suggested the tier structure in (1) for Javanese consonants.

(1)
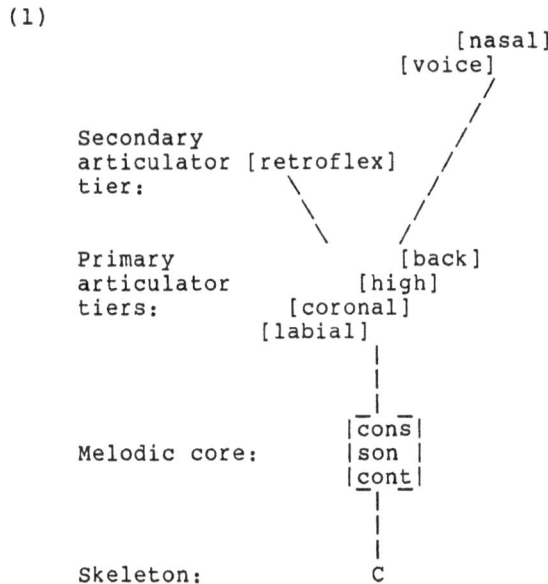

The representations for the Javanese consonants are given in (2).

(2)
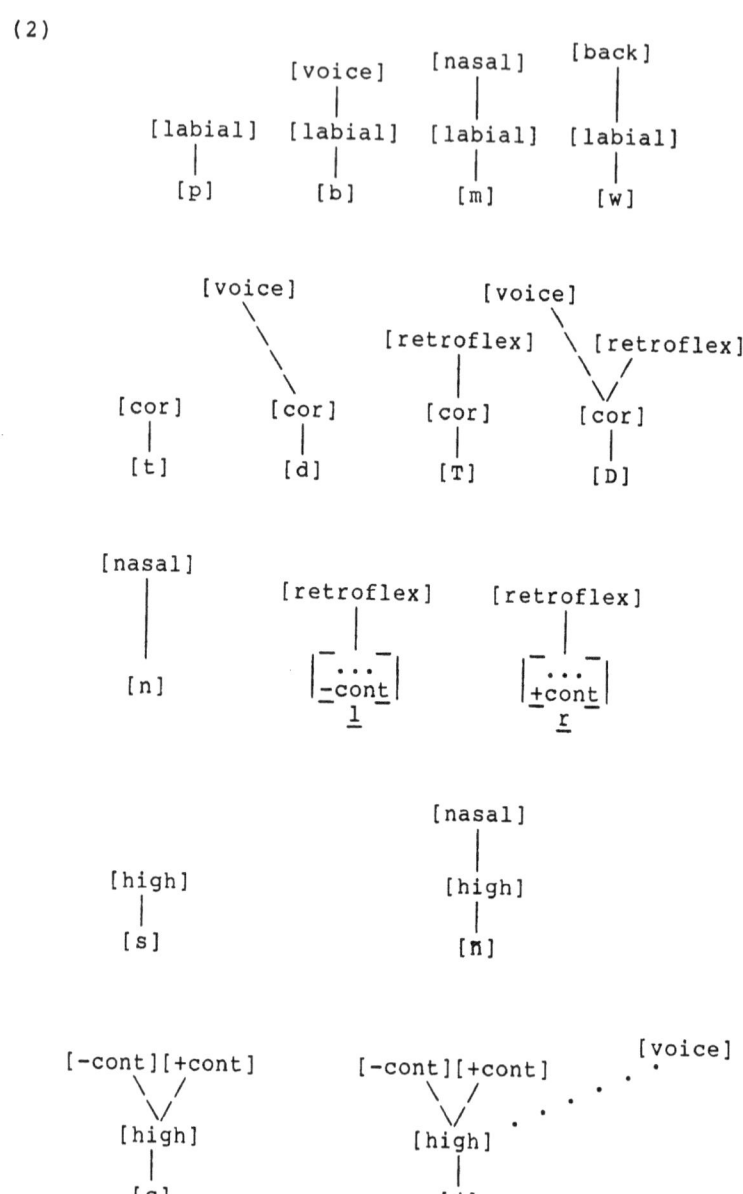

The dependency of voicing, nasality, and retroflexion on the primary articulator features accounts for the incompatibility of homorganic consonants within morphemes.

The assumption that the primary articulator features each occupy a separate tier finds support in the existence of long-distance OCP effects.

We have suggested that coronal sonorants are underlyingly unspecified for coronality and can therefore cooccur with coronal obstruents in morphemes.

As a specific Javanese constraint, we have proposed that the feature [retroflex] is governed by a branching prohibition (repeated in (3)).

(3)
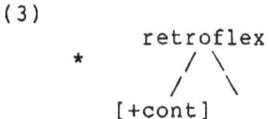

The explanation for the Javanese morpheme structure constraints proposed in this chapter rests on a high degree of tier articulation. An important issue which arises in this context is the universality and derivational persistence of such maximal differentiation of tiers. The fact that not all languages possess root constraints like Javanese or Semitic strongly argues that this is a language-specific option. In particular, the segregation of consonantal and vocalic melodies onto different tiers is a parameter set by individual languages. The Javanese evidence shows that this basic split of the melody tier is not always grounded in the morphological system in the way it is in Semitic languages (see also Prince 1986 for discussion on this point). Furthermore, the tier structures necessary to explain morpheme structure are not isomorphic to those demanded by the phonology. It seems that languages with maximal initial differentiation partially conflate tiers before the phonological derivation starts. This is not Tier Conflation in the sense of erasure of morphological bracketing, but in the more general sense of reduction of structural complexity. Thus the separate articulator tiers are folded together into a single place tier, and dependent ordering of tiers is reduced. We thus come to recognize a distinction between 'root structure' or 'morpheme structure', i.e. the repository of the basic morphemes of a language, and the lexicon at large, where morphological and phonological operations on the basic morphemes are performed. The thesis is that the tier configurations found in morpheme structure and in the later phonology can differ, the latter being the result of partial conflation of initially autonomous tiers. To put it briefly, all languages simplify tier structure at certain points of the derivation. Many languages already start out with conflated tiers in morpheme structure, they therefore have no (or few) root constraints. Other languages start out with a highly articulated tier structure, which entails the existence of root constraints; such languages partially conflate tiers at the beginning of the phonological derivation.

2.7 Appendix:

Cooccurrence Statistics for Javanese Consonants

This appendix presents a statistical analysis of the consonant cooccurrence restrictions in Javanese and supplies the empirical foundation for the analysis presented in this chapter.

The distribution of consonants in C_1 and C_2 in Javanese morphemes of the form $C_1VC_2VC_3$ is given in Table I (on the next page repeated from section 2.0). To determine which phoneme cooccurrences are significantly rare, we have to weigh, for each phoneme combination, the actual number of cooccurrences against the expected number of occurrences. The latter is calculated in the standard way. Each phoneme combination corresponds to one cell in the matrix in Table I. For the cell in row_i and in $column_j$, the expected value is calculated as in (1).

(1)
$$\frac{\text{total of row}_i * \text{total of column}_j}{\text{grand total}}$$

Table I   Javanese C1/C2   Occurrences

C1\C2	p	b	m	w	t	d	T	D	r	l	n	ñ	s	c	j	y	k	g	ḍ	h	S
p	41	1	9	8	39	7	49	21	64	75	24	4	41	43	17	19	46	26	24	8	566
b	6	45	0	22	28	8	19	48	60	74	24	6	32	21	27	23	29	20	32	4	528
m	4	9	18	15	11	21	16	13	39	44	26	25	19	7	19	20	10	30	23	8	377
w	2	1	0	23	18	18	2	19	31	43	14	1	10	2	22	13	10	9	6	0	244
t	38	29	21	24	46	3	0	15	50	63	19	0	10	0	9	17	40	27	18	5	434
d	3	10	22	7	1	17	0	0	14	39	7	1	3	0	0	5	12	7	3	1	152
T	0	0	7	5	0	0	10	0	8	8	2	0	1	0	0	5	9	0	11	0	66
D	14	5	13	20	3	0	1	32	7	10	5	1	11	5	1	13	29	9	12	9	200
r	28	29	30	37	15	5	0	3	16	4	6	8	20	16	30	35	17	36	18	3	356
l	22	27	42	49	21	13	16	23	68	35	15	14	26	16	17	34	28	30	28	11	535
n	3	1	4	0	5	1	0	1	1	0	13	0	5	2	5	3	7	2	2	4	60
ñ	1	2	8	0	1	0	3	1	4	0	2	9	0	0	0	1	0	3	4	0	39
ŋ	35	34	38	52	26	11	17	33	76	76	24	0	43	1	8	27	39	30	43	7	620
c	31	21	25	39	7	1	30	15	42	40	11	0	0	43	2	7	54	17	35	2	422
j	10	39	22	26	12	11	7	27	36	29	17	0	3	1	20	6	12	28	10	1	317
y	0	0	0	0	3	0	0	0	1	0	0	0	0	0	0	3	2	1	0	0	9
k	64	37	32	55	55	34	54	32	83	96	39	29	46	50	23	37	46	7	8	3	830
g	23	44	23	25	30	15	38	37	64	59	20	11	27	23	22	22	1	42	0	1	527
ḍ	1	5	1	5	2	2	4	0	9	3	7	6	3	5	2	5	8	1	3	1	73
S	326	339	315	412	323	167	266	320	672	699	275	115	300	235	224	295	399	325	280	68	6355

The expected frequencies constitute a null hypothesis for a significance test. I have used a non-parametric significance test, the chi-square test (henceforth x^2). The goal is to determine, for each phoneme combination, whether or not its observed number of occurrences is significantly smaller than its expected number of occurrences. The results of the x^2 test for each phoneme combination are given in Table II (on the next page).

The x^2 values in Table II and in all following tables translate (on one degree of freedom) into probabilities or significance levels as indicated in (2).

(2)

x^2 value	Significance Level
$x^2 > 3.84$	$p < 0.05$
$x^2 > 5.02$	$p < 0.025$
$x^2 > 6.64$	$p < 0.01$
$x^2 > 10.83$	$p < 0.001$

x^2 values > 3.84 indicate (on one degree of freedom) significance at the 0.05 level, i.e. there are only 5 chances in 100 that the deviation is due to chance, etc. Table II lists only x^2 values > 3.84, i.e. cases where the deviation of the actual number of occurrences from the expected number of occurrences is significant at least at the 0.05 level.

Table II   Javanese C1/C2   chi square values

	p	b	m	w	t	d	T	D	r	l	n	s	c	j	y	k	g	ṭ	h
p		28.23	12.94	22.44															
b			16.41	26.17	4.37														
m				12.17	6.14														
w					8.84	11.09	12.09						5.47			7.89			
t							6.19	18.17											
d					5.86			6.36	7.65				5.62	5.36					
T							6.60												
D					5.05	9.26	6.49		9.47	6.54				5.19					
r							14.90	12.43	12.45	31.57	5.74								
l										9.66									
n																			
ṇ												7.85	5.37	16.05					
s											11.22		20.97	8.78					
c					9.73	9.18					7.64	19.92		11.14	8.09				
j											5.74	9.57	9.81		5.16				
y																			
k																	29.60	22.32	
g																31.12		23.22	
ṭ																			

I have left out x^2 values for those phoneme combinations whose expected frequency is very low, since the x^2 test is known to be unreliable and misleading in such cases. This concerns combinations with initial $\underline{T}$, $\underline{n}$, $\underline{ñ}$, $\underline{ṇ}$, and $\underline{y}$.

The x^2 test determines the significance of the deviation of the observed value from the expected value in both directions, positive and negative. We are here interested only in those combinations which occur significantly _less_ frequently than expected, i.e. cases where phonemes exclude each other. Therefore I have discarded the x^2 values of all those combinations which occur _more_ frequently than expected. In this way Table II unambiguously expresses significantly low frequency of phoneme cooccurrence.

2.7.1 Labials

The following tables (3a-c) illustrate cooccurrences of labials in C_1/C_2. Table (3a) gives the actual number of cooccurrences for each pair of labial consonants. C_1 is represented vertically, C_2 horizontally. Table (3b) contains the expected cooccurrence frequency for each pair, and Table (3c) shows the x^2 values for the labial combinations.

(3) a. Occurrences:

c_1 \ c_2	p	b	m	w
p	41	1	9	8
b	6	45	0	22
m	4	9	18	15
w	2	1	0	23

b. Expected Values:

c_1 \ c_2	p	b	m	w
p	29.03	30.19	28.06	36.69
b	27.09	28.17	26.17	34.23
m	19.34	20.11	18.69	24.44
w	12.52	13.02	12.09	15.82

c. x^2 Distribution:

c_1 \ c_2	p	b	m	w
p		28.23	12.94	22.44
b	16.41		26.17	4.37
m	12.17	6.14		
w	8.84	11.09	12.09	

x^2:	>3.84	>6.64	>10.83
p:	<0.05	<0.01	<0.001

As can be seen in (3c), almost all combinations of different labials are excluded on high levels of significance. None of the combinations of identical labials is excluded, however, and the diagonal of the x^2 table shows no entries. Summing up the x^2 values of the whole labial matrix, we find that the dissociative interaction of labials is significant $p < 0.001$.

There is only a single combination of nonidentical

labials which is not significantly rare, namely initial m cooccurring with medial w.

2.7.2 Palatals

The exclusion relations in C_1/C_2 among the segments s, c, j, and ñ are given in the following tables.[1]

(4)
    a. Occurrences:

C_1\C_2	s	c	j	ñ
s	43	1	8	0
c	0	43	2	0
j	3	1	20	0
ñ	0	0	0	9

    b. Expected Values:

C_1\C_2	s	c	j	ñ
s	29.27	22.93	21.85	11.22
c	19.92	15.61	14.87	7.64
j	14.96	11.72	11.17	5.74
ñ	1.44	1.37	1.84	.71

---

[1] The glide y has been omitted in (4) since it is only weakly integrated into the system; y is vanishingly rare in initial position, and in C_2 it shows some interaction with initial c and j, but not with s.

c. x^2 values:

C_1 \ C_2	s	c	j	ñ
s		20.97	8.78	11.22
c	19.92		11.14	7.64
j	9.57	9.81		5.74
ñ	−	−	−	−

x^2:	>3.84	>6.64	>10.83
p:	<0.05	<0.01	<0.001

Identical palatals are permitted in C_1/C_2, every other combination of palatals is significantly excluded. There are 15 divergent cases, 11 of them involve s and j in either order. The table of expected frequencies (4b) indicates that the palatal nasal ñ is overall too rare in initial position (but not in C_2) to calculate x^2 values. (I have indicated this here and in the following tables by entering a minus sign in the appropriate cells of the x^2 table.) It is worth noting, however, that all of the 9 cases with initial ñ in the above table are of the 'geminate' type ññ, there is no cooccurrence with another palatal in C_2 position.

2.7.3 Velars

Tables (5a-c) present the cooccurrence statistics for velar consonants in C_1/C_2.

(5)   a.   Occurrences:

C_1 \ C_2	k	g	ŋ
k	46	7	8
g	1	42	0
ŋ	8	1	3

b.   Expected values:

C_1 \ C_2	k	g	ŋ
k	52.11	42.45	36.57
g	33.09	26.96	23.22
ŋ	4.58	3.73	3.22

c. X^2 values:

C_1 \ C_2	k	g	ŋ
k		29.60	22.32
g	31.12		23.22
ŋ	-	-	-

X^2: >3.84	>6.64	>10.83
p: <0.05	<0.01	< 0.001

Initial ŋ is overall too rare to draw any conclusions. In the clear cases, all combinations of nonidentical velars are significantly excluded in C_1/C_2.

2.7.4 Coronal Obstruents

The cooccurrence of coronal obstruents is severely restricted, as shown by the following tables for C_1/C_2. Retroflex $\underline{T}$ is too infrequent in initial position (expected frequency < 5 for all combinations) to draw any conclusions from its combinatorial behavior.

(6)
a. Occurrences:

C_1 \ C_2	t	d	T	D
t	46	3	0	15
d	1	17	0	0
T	0	0	10	0
D	3	0	1	32

b. Expected values:

C_1 \ C_2	t	d	T	D
t	22.06	11.40	18.17	21.85
d	7.73	3.99	6.39	7.65
T	3.35	1.73	2.76	3.32
D	10.17	5.26	8.37	10.07

c. X^2 values:

C_1 \ C_2	t	d	T	D
t		6.19	18.17	
d	5.86		6.36	7.65
T	-	-	-	-
D	5.05	5.26	6.49	

X^2: >3.84	>6.64	>10.83
p: <0.05	<0.01	< 0.001

The pattern of coronal incompatibility is very clear and has only one minor exception: Combinations of initial t medial retroflex D are not significantly restricted and constitute 15 of the 23 occurring combinations of nonidenticals. Notice that the opposite order Dt is unremarkable, there are only 3 occurrences.

2.7.5 Combinations involving the root-final position

Consonants occupying the final position in a morpheme do not show consistent OCP-interactions with preceding tautomorphemic consonants. Consider for example the cooccurrences of coronal obstruents in C_2/C_3, which are tabulated in (7).[2]

---

[2] In (7), t appears as the only C_3 coronal. The retroflex stops T and D do not occur at the end of a morpheme, but Standard Javanese allows underlying d in morpheme-final position, which is devoiced word-finally. However, Uhlenbeck (1949) based his counts on the isolation form of morphemes, in which both underlying d and t appear as t.

(7)

Occurrences: Expected values: x^2 values:

C_2\\$^{C_3}$ t   t   t
        ------   ------   ------
    t| 8   t| 41.58   t| 27.12
    d| 18   d| 21.37   d|
    T| 37   T| 34.37   T|
    D| 33   D| 41.20   D|

As shown by the x^2 distribution, d, T, and D in medial position do not interact with final t. On the other hand, the identity combination tt is significantly rare.

In C_1/C_3, we find the following cooccurrences of coronal obstruents:

(8)

Occurrences: Expected values: x^2 values:

C_1\\$^{C_3}$ t   t   t
        ------   ------   ------
    t| 24   t| 55.92   t| 18.22
    d| 8   d| 19.58   d| 6.85
    T| 2   T| 8.50   T| 4.97
    D| 27   D| 25.77   D|

| x^2: >3.84 | >6.64 | >10.83 |
| p: <0.05 | <0.01 | < 0.001 |

It is true that all combinations of coronal obstruents except Dt are significantly rare, but the exclusion effects are not very strong for dt and Tt, and there is a large number (24 out of 55.92 expected) of tt combinations.

Relatively consistent OCP-interactions involving the root-final position are found among the labials. Table (9) shows the cooccurrence statistics for labials in C_2/C_3.

(9)

a. Occurrences:

C_2 \ C_3	p	m
p	2	1
b	8	0
m	3	1
w	5	1

b. Expected Values:

C_2 \ C_3	p	m
p	12.83	7.64
b	13.34	7.95
m	12.39	7.39
w	16.21	9.66

c. X^2 Values:

C_2 \ C_3	p	m
p	9.14	5.78
b		7.95
m	7.12	5.52
w	7.75	7.76

X^2:	>3.84	>6.64	>10.83
p:	<0.05	<0.01	<0.001

Labials are not very frequent in final position, the table with the expected frequencies (9c) shows this quite clearly. Even so, the X^2 table indicates that almost all combination of labials (except for bp) are significantly excluded. This cannot just be attributed to the fact that labials are relatively rare in final position, because the frequency factor is explicitly taken into account in the computation of the x^2 values. The most important finding is that both identical and nonidentical labials are barred from cooccurring in C_2/C_3.

Table (10) summarizes the cooccurrence statistics for labials in C_1/C_3, i.e. for nonadjacent combinations of morpheme-initial labials with morpheme-final labials.

(10)
    a. Occurrences:

C_1\C_3	p	m
p	0	7
b	3	12
m	7	11
w	2	1

    b. Expected values:

C_1\C_3	p	m
p	22.29	13.28
b	20.79	12.39
m	14.92	8.89
w	9.57	5.70

c. x^2 values:

```
 \c_3    p         m
c_1    ---------------
   p|  22.29
   b|  15.22
   m|   4.21
   w|   5.99      (3.88)
```

Correction for continuity[3]: x^2 (w/m) = 3.09

x^2: >3.84	>6.64	>10.83
p: <0.05	<0.01	< 0.001

Combinations of initial labials with final p are all significantly excluded, and in particular the dissociative relations between initial p b and final p are highly significant. On the other hand, combinations of initial labials with final m are not significantly rare. It is quite possible, however, that this is only an apparent violation of the labial cooccurrence restriction: Uhlenbeck (1949, 115-7) indicates that in a substantial number of cases final m seems to constitute a separate morpheme. If this is the case, such cooccurrences of final m with other labials are irrelevant for our purposes.

---

[3] The combination w-m has a low expected frequency, and the correction for continuity given above shows that it is not significantly excluded at the 0.05 level.

2.7.6 Liquids

2.7.6.1 Liquids in C_1/C_2

(11)
a. Occurrences:

C_1\\C_2	l	r
l	35	68
r	4	16

b. Expected values:

C_1\\C_2	l	r
l	58.85	56.57
r	39.16	37.64

c. X_2 values:

C_1\\C_2	l	r
l	9.66	
r	31.57	12.45

X^2:	>3.84	>6.64	>10.83
p:	<0.05	<0.01	<0.001

It is immediately apparent that lr is the only unquestionably admitted liquid combination. It occurs in 68 cases, including many native Javanese morphemes like l@r@n 'stop, rest', laraṅ 'expensive', or l@r@s 'correct'. The combination ll is significantly rare ($X^2 = 9.66$, i.e. $p < 0.01$), but it occurs in too many forms (35) to be dismissed as exceptional. Most of the forms with ll are native Javanese morphemes like leleh 'soft' or lali 'forget'. The combination rl, on the other hand, does not occur in native Javanese morphemes, and its exclusion is highly significant ($X^2 = 31.57$, i.e. $p < 0.001$). Sporadic cases with this combination are either unassimilated loans from Dutch like rolah 'rollag' and rolis 'rollijst' or are clearly polymorphemic like ro-las 'twelve (two-teen)'. The combination rr is also significantly rare, but it occurs in 16 morphemes. Uhlenbeck (1949, 128-9) points out the interesting fact that most of these morphemes have doublets with the dissimilated form lr. Table (12) gives a representative list of such doublets.

(12)
```
    rarab       'regen (in de avond)'            larab
    raras       'klank, harmonie'                laras
    r@r@m       'tot bedagen komen'              l@r@m
    reren       'stilhouden'                     leren
    ririh       'zachtjes'                       lirih
    rirep       'ongedeerd'                      lirip
    rurub       'bedeckt als met 'n kleed'       lurup
    rurus       'fraai, recht'                   lurus
    rarah       'verspreid liggend afval'        larah
    ruruh       '(op)gezocht'                    luruh
```

The forms in (12) indicate that a liquid dissimilation process has operated in the history of the Javanese language, changing the sequence rr into lr. In fact, this dissimilatory sound change, which distinguishes Modern Javanese from Old Javanese and from other Western

Austronesian languages like Sundanese, is well established on comparative grounds (see e.g. Nothofer 1975, 104-5) and was already postulated in the earliest work on comparative Austronesian grammar (see Dempwolff 1934, 36).

In terms of the analysis presented in this chapter, the dissimilated forms have undergone a historical reanalysis and no longer involve core spreading (as in (13a)), but two separate liquid cores units (as is (13b)).

(13)

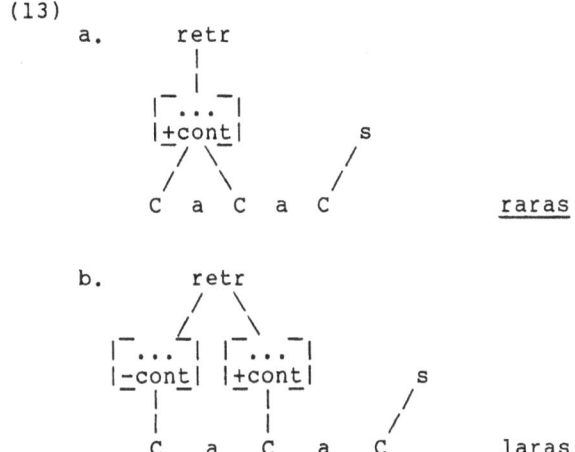

To sum up, in C_1/C_2 the liquid sequence rl is clearly excluded and the sequence lr clearly admitted. The identity combinations ll and rr both occur in a fair number of cases, with the the number of combinations of the latter kind reduced by an historical liquid dissimilation process.

2.7.6.2 _Liquids in C_2/C_3_

The distribution of liquids in C_2/C_3 is distinctly different from the one encountered in C_1/C_2, as can be seen from the following tables.

(14)   a.   Occurrences:

C_2\\$^{C_3}$	l	r
l	7	77
r	4	1

b.   Expected values:

C_2\\$^{C_3}$	l	r
l	58.44	72.61
r	56.26	69.91

c. x^2 values:

C_2\\$^{C_3}$	l	r
l	45.28	
r	48.55	67.92

x^2:	>3.84	>6.64	>10.83
p:	<0.05	<0.01	< 0.001

The liquid combination _lr_ is again clearly admitted, as it was in C_1/C_2. It is the most frequent combination and occurs in 77 morphemes (e.g. _tular_ 'infect', _tilar_ 'leave', _g@lar_ 'spread'). The combination _ll_ does not occur in native morphemes in C_2/C_3, this is quite different from C_1/C_2. Its x^2 value (45.28) is highly significant. Uhlenbeck (1949, 129) points out that the few existing cases are Arabic loan words like <u>bilal</u> 'afroepen van de tijden voor de godsdienstoefeningen', <u>kalal</u> 'door de wet geoorloofd', <u>palal</u> 'gunst van God', and <u>jalal</u> 'heerlijkheid Gods'. The combination <u>rl</u> is inadmissible in C_2/C_3 for native morphemes, its x^2 value is highly significant (x^2 = 48.55). Among the four cases appearing in the table are two loans (<u>parol</u> 'parool, wachtwoord' from Dutch and <u>ṅaral</u> 'beletsel' from Arabic). The combination <u>rr</u> finally is totally excluded in C_2/C_3, it occurs only in one loanword from Dutch (<u>purir</u> 'fourier').

We can conclude that the only liquid combination admitted in C_2/C_3 is <u>lr</u>.

2.7.6.3 Liquids in C_1/C_3

In C_1/C_3 we find basically the same distribution of liquids as in C_2/C_3. The only difference lies in the fact that there are more cases of the sequence <u>rl</u>, witness the following tables.

(15)
    a. Occurrences:

c_1 \ c_3	l	r
l	1	75
r	29	0

    b. Expected values:

c_1 \ c_3	l	r
l	44.83	55.62
r	29.33	36.38

    c. x^2 values:

c_1 \ c_3	l	r
l	42.85	
r		36.38

x^2:	>3.84	>6.64	>10.83
p:	<0.05	<0.01	<0.001

The tables show that lr is again clearly admitted, it is the most frequent combination and occurs in 75 morphemes. The combinations ll and rr are both excluded on high levels of significance, as in C_2/C_3. The first occurs only in a single loanword from Arabic (lapal 'tekst'), the second not at all. The case of rl is more complicated. The constraint against the sequence rl which is observed in C_1/C_2 and in C_2/C_3 is more frequently broken in C_1/C_3. In fact, this sequence is not significantly excluded and occurs in 29 morphemes. Uhlenbeck (1949, 129) notes, however, that most of these 29 cases are of a special character, consisting of loans from Arabic, Dutch, and Portuguese, or of morphemes of dialectal origin. (16) is an almost exhaustive list of these morphemes.

(16)
   a. Loans from Arabic:

       ramal   'waarzegging'
       rapal   'tekst' (occurs also as lapal)
       rasul   'gezant Gods'
       rekal   'leeslessenaar'

   b. Loans from Durch:

       r@bal   'proces-verbaal'
       rog@l   'orgel'
       riwil   'vrijwil'
       royal   'doordraaier, losbol'
       ropel   'dubbel'

   c. From Portuguese:

       reyal   'reaal'

   d. Dialectal morphemes:

       rebel \
       regel \
       rigal   \
       rigel   } 'afvallen'
       rigol /
       rugul /
       rogol/

       regol   'potsenmaker'
       riyol   'ruil' (Standard Javanese iyol)
       rumil   'zaniken'
       rokel   'hobbelig'
       romal   'hoofddoek'

2.7.7 Retroflex stops and /r/

There is one significant exclusion relation between coronal obstruents and coronal sonorants. As Table (17) shows, cooccurrences of the liquid r in initial position with retroflex obstruents T D in C_2 are excluded on high levels of significance. There are no forms with rT and only 3 forms with rD.

(17) a. Occurrences:

C_1 \ C_2	T	D
r	0	3

b. Expected Values:

C_1 \ C_2	T	D
r	14.90	17.93

c. X^2 values:

C_1 \ C_2	T	D
r	14.90	12.43

X^2:	>3.84	>6.64	>10.83
p:	<0.05	<0.01	<0.001

It is highly dubious whether the opposite order (T, D preceding r) is also excluded. Consider first the cooccurrence statistics for C_1/C_2 in (18).

(18)

    Occurrences: Expected values: x^2 values:

```
   \c2       r                    r                  r
 c1\      ------              ------             ------
       T|   8               T|   6.98          T|    -
       D|   7               D|  21.15          D|   9.47
```

Initial $\underline{T}$ is too rare to draw any firm conclusions, but note that there are 8 occurrences of $\underline{Tr}$, which exceeds the expected value (6.98). The combination $\underline{Dr}$ is significantly rare, but there are 7 occurrences.

Secondly, the combinations of morpheme-final $\underline{r}$ with medial and initial $\underline{T}$, $\underline{D}$ appear entirely unrestricted, cf. (19) and (20), respectively. None of these combinations is significantly rare.

(19)

    Occurrences: Expected values: x^2 values:

```
   \c3       r                    r                  r
 c2\      ------              ------             ------
       T|  21               T|  27.78          T|
       D|  28               D|  33.29          D|
```

(20)

    Occurrences: Expected values: x^2 values:

```
   \c3       r                    r                  r
 c1\      ------              ------             ------
       T|   8               T|   6.86          T|    -
       D|  19               D|  20.79          D|
```

Since the retroflex stops do not occur at all in morpheme-final position, cooccurrences of initial or medial r̲ with final T̲, D̲ are impossible irrespective of any cooccurrence restriction.

On the basis of these facts I interpret the interaction of r̲ with T̲ and D̲ as asymmetric, holding only in the order r̲ + {T̲,D̲}. Since l̲ is also retroflex in Javanese, this restriction can be combined with the restriction against the liquid sequence *rl by stating that r + retroflex is quite generally ruled out.

2.7.8 Coronal/palatal cooccurrences

Uhlenbeck (1949, 122-3) observed that the combinatorial restrictions holding between coronals and palatals are somewhat special in that they are directional. His generalization is that the order coronal + palatal does not occur very often, whereas the order palatal + coronal is quite usual. A statistical analysis of the cooccurrence data for C_1/C_2 shows that the facts are not quite so clear (see the tables in (21) and (22)), still Uhlenbeck's generalization holds as a tendency: There are more combinatorial restrictions in the order coronal + palatal (21c) than in the order palatal + coronal (22c).

(21) Coronal + Palatal

a. Occurrences:

c_1\\c_2	ñ	s	c	j
t	0	10	0	9
d	1	3	0	0
T	0	0	0	0
D	1	11	5	1

b. Expected Values:

c_1\\c_2	ñ	s	c	j
t	7.85	20.49	16.05	15.30
d	2.75	7.18	5.62	5.36
T	1.19	3.12	2.44	2.33
D	3.62	9.44	7.40	7.05

c. x^2 Values:

c_1\\c_2	ñ	s	c	j
t	7.85	5.37	16.05	
d	–		5.62	5.36
T	–	–	–	
D	–			5.19

x^2:	>3.84	>6.64	>10.83
p:	<0.05	<0.01	<0.001

(22) Palatal + Coronal

a. Occurrences

c_1\\c_2	t	d	T	D
ñ	1	0	3	1
s	26	11	17	33
c	7	1	30	15
j	12	11	7	27

b. Expected values:

C_1\\C_2	t	d	T	D
n	1.98	1.02	1.63	1.96
s	31.51	16.29	25.95	31.22
c	21.45	11.09	17.66	21.25
j	16.11	8.33	13.27	15.96

c. X^2 Values:

C_1\\C_2	t	d	T	D
n	-	-	-	-
s				
c	9.73	9.18		
j				

X^2:	>3.84	>6.64	>10.83
p:	<0.05	<0.01	<0.001

In keeping with the feature representations which we have assumed in this chapter, we could implement the coronal-palatal restriction by a special sequential constraint, as in (23).

(23)
```
     * coronal
       |      high
       |       |
     [core] [core]
```

The constraint in (23) is a separate stipulation and has nothing to do with the OCP.

CHAPTER III

MELODY ASSOCIATION IN REDUPLICATION

3.0 *Introduction*

After having discussed some aspects of the internal structure of melody elements, I will turn to certain questions regarding the external relations of melody units to skeletal elements in this chapter. One of the fundamental tenets of CV phonology (cf. Clements and Keyser 1983 and work cited there) is that the relationship between melody elements and skeleton slots is not restricted to biuniqueness, but can be one-to-many (e.g. in long vowels) or many-to-one (e.g. in short diphthongs). Thus the set of possible melody-skeleton relations is simply determined by the theory of association, which allows nonbiuniqueness but prohibits line crossing. Spreading of melody elements to adjacent skeleton positions is possible, but nonadjacent positions are inaccessible whenever other associated melody elements intervene. The associative range for melody elements which is directly made available in this way appears insufficient in one respect, however, and an additional principle of melody copying was admitted into the theory to fill the perceived gap. The problem arises in reduplicative constructions if we adopt the basic hypothesis (McCarthy 1979, 1981, Marantz 1982) that reduplication involves purely skeletal affixes, composed of C and V elements devoid of phonemic content, which are dependent for their phonemic filling on the base to which they are attached. In the typical case more than a single skeletal slot has to be provided with a phonemic melody. If this were done by linear spreading of the stem melody, it would inevitably lead to line crossing, as schematically indicated in (1) for a reduplicative prefix of the form CVC.

(1)
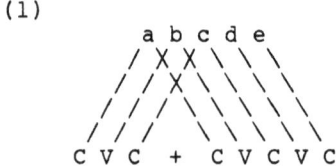
```
            a b c d e
           / X X \ \ \
          / / X \ \ \ \
         / / / \ \ \ \ \
        / / /   \ \ \ \ \
       C V C  +  C V C V C
```

Note that splitting the melody into consonantal and vocalic melodies does not help in the general case, because the problem persists in the separate consonant and vowel planes if more than a single consonantal or vocalic melody element must be associated with the reduplicative template.

In the first systematic study of reduplication in the framework of CV phonology, Marantz (1982), building on the work of McCarthy (1979, 1981), proposed a universal principle of melody copying to deal with this problem. Marantz's (1982) theory is briefly illustrated in (2), taking plural formation in Agta as an example. In Agta, certain kinds of plurals are formed by reduplicating the first consonant - vowel - consonant sequence of the root. Thus the plural of takki 'leg' is tak-takki 'legs'.

(2)
    a.   Prefixation of CVC skeleton:

```
              t a   k i
              | |  /\ |
      C V C + C V C C V
```
                                                    takki   'leg'

    b.   Melody Copying:

```
      t a k i   t a   k i
                | |  /\ |
      C V C  +  C V C C V
```

    c.   Association:

```
      t a k i   t a   k i
      | | |     | |  /\ |
      C V C  +  C V C C V
```
                                                     tak-takki 'legs'

In Marantz's (1982) approach, the derivation of reduplicated forms takes place in three steps:

(i)   The reduplicative morpheme, a purely skeletal affix, is affixed (in this case: prefixed) to the root, like any other affix (2a).

(ii)   The phonemic melody of the root is copied 'over' the skeletal affix (2b). This copying operation is not a transformation which is part of a particular grammar. Rather, it is a universal operation automatically triggered by affixes without melody.[1]

(iii) The copied phonemic melody is associated with the C and V slots of the reduplicative affix (2c). In the unmarked case, association takes place left-to-right for prefixes and right-to-left for suffixes. Elements which are left over after association are discarded, and we end up with the desired form <u>tak-takki</u> 'legs'.

There are a number of conceptual considerations which can be adduced against the Copying Theory. Note first that the postulation of a melody copying operation introduces a reduplication-specific mechanism, and this is undesirable in the context of the overall program of assimilating reduplication to other affixational processes as much as possible, reducing the reduplication-specific elements of the theory to the absolute minimum. Secondly, wholescale melody copying duplicates more melodic material than is needed for association, and the unused melody elements have to be discarded. This is in itself not a

---

[1] McCarthy (1981) points out that a feature triggering copying is necessary because there are cases of purely skeletal affixes which induce linear spreading and not copying. Such affixes occur e.g. in Semitic (McCarthy 1979, 1981) and in Ancient Greek (Steriade 1982).

problem, because we can appeal to the general and independently motivated procedure of Stray Erasure (McCarthy 1979, Steriade 1982). The slightly troublesome aspect of total copying lies rather in in the fact that unused copied material in reduplication appears never to have any phonological effects and therefore has to be discarded immediately. This is different from unassociated melody elements encountered outside of reduplication, which have been found to have phonological consequences at later points of the derivation for example in vowel harmony systems (Clements 1977, 1981, Kenstowicz 1979). In the general case, then, Stray Erasure is assumed to apply at the end of a level (or even postlexically) and not immediately when a stray element is encountered.

Such conceptual considerations, although they do not carry decisive weight in themselves, invite the exploration of alternatives to the Copying Theory. More importantly, the Copying Theory of reduplication encounters empirical problems in the interaction of reduplication with phonological rules, generally known under the headings "overapplication" and "underapplication" of rules (this terminology is due to Wilbur 1973, who first studied these phenomena systematically in a generative framework). I will argue that these phenomena support another approach to the association problem in reduplication, an approach which does not have a copying mechanism.

The empirical problem I will focus on is the fact that reduplication as a morphological operation often interacts with phonological rules in a rather unexpected way. The problem was first pointed out in Bloomfield (1933: 222) and extensively discussed in Wilbur (1973). I will illustrate the point with the example used by Bloomfield in his original discussion, namely the interaction of Nasal Substitution and Reduplication in Tagalog. Like other Western Austronesian languages, Tagalog has a rule of Nasal Substitution by which, among other things, the final nasal of certain prefixes replaces a following root-initial voiceless obstruent, acquiring its place of articulation. Nasals undergoing this rule will be represented by the nasal archisegment N. Nasal Substitution is illustrated in (3) for the root ta:kot 'to frighten' and the prefix maN, where the sequence Nt is replaced by n.

(3)

	ta:kot	maN+ta:kot
Nasal Substitution:		ma na:kot
	'frighten'	'frighten several people'

Tagalog forms gerunds by reduplicating the initial CV sequence of the root and prefixing the nasal-substituting prefix paN, in that order. When nasal-substituting prefixes combine with reduplicated forms in this way, something unexpected happens. As shown in (4), Nasal Substitution applies to both parts of the reduplicative construction, although the triggering nasal is adjacent to only one part. In the terminology of Wilbur (1973), the rule of Nasal Substitution "overapplies".

(4)   paN + C V + ta:kot -->   pa + na + na:kot
                                   *pa + na + ta:kot
                                   'frightening'

I will argue that overapplication and underapplication of phonological rules find a natural explanation in another approach to the association problem in reduplication, an approach which does not use a copying mechanism. The basic hypothesis that I want to explore takes up the idea proposed (largely independently) in a number of studies[2] that reduplication is a nonconcatenative construction in which the base and its (partial or total) reduplicate are underlyingly represented in parallel and not in sequence.

---

[2]See Georgopoulos (1982), Plenat (1982), Kitagawa (1984, to appear), Cowper and Rice (1985), Clements (1985), Levin (1985), Uhrbach (1985), McCarthy (ms.); cf. also earlier work by Hirschbühler (1978) on across-the-board (ATB) representation of reduplicative constructions in an SPE-style framework and suggestions about ATB-representation in stress theory attributed to Roger Higgins in Prince (1983, 45-6).

This idea has found various formal expressions. Hirschbühler (1978) considers an ATB representation of reduplication in an SPE-style framework. Kitagawa (1984, to appear) argues that reduplication is a rule which copies part of the base skeleton onto another parallel tier, preserving its association with the melody. Other proposals have tried to combine the successful affixational approach to reduplication with the idea of parallel representation, conceiving of the reduplicative skeleton not as a linear affix but as a morpheme <u>synchronous</u> with the root skeleton, like the consonantal and vocalic melodies in Semitic languages familiar from McCarthy's (1979, 1981) work. Clements (1985) proposes a skeleton-to-skeleton association between the synchronous reduplicative and base skeleta, and Uhrbach (1985) an ATB representation. It has been pointed out, most explicitly in Uhrbach (1985), that a 'parallel' representation of this general kind might provide an answer to the problem of rule overapplication. In what follows I will take up this line of thought and develop it in a certain direction. In particular, I suggest that the only basic modification needed in Marantz's (1982) framework is the recognition of synchronous skeletal morphemes, all other aspects of the theory remain the same. Thus I assume that the skeleton is an <u>affix</u>, albeit a synchronous one. I also suggest that the reduplicative skeleton is associated with the _melody_ of the root[3] and not, as in Clements (1985), with the _skeleton_ of the root. Association between reduplicative skeleton and melody proceeds in the usual (phoneme-driven) way. There is of course no melody copying in this theory, since the melody of the root is entirely accessible for association to the reduplicative skeleton. For ease of reference, I will call this the "Single Melody Theory" of reduplication. The general approach is illustrated in (5), using Tagalog CV reduplication as an example. In (5) the skeletal CV affix is introduced on a separate tier and associated left-to-right with the root melody.

(5)
```
        C V
        | |
        l a k a d         la-la:kad    'walking'
        |/\ | | |
        C V V C V C
```

Some remarks are in order here on my use of C's and V's as skeletal units. Since I am not primarily concerned with questions regarding the internal composition of the skeleton, I will for expository simplicity employ the familiar CV-notation. The approach presented here is however clearly compatible with more recent developments

---

[3]This seems to be essentially also the approach in Plenat (1982).

in skeleton theory such as the X-skeleton proposed by Levin (1983, 1985) and in particular with the prosodic skeleton theory proposed by McCarthy and Prince in recent work (McCarthy and Prince 1985, in prep.), according to which prosodic templates are built out of the independently justified units of prosody (e.g. word, foot, syllable, mora) and not out of units like C, V, or X which correspond to the traditional notion 'segment'. In certain instances I will deviate from my strategy of typographical conservatism and adopt moraic/syllabic representations in cases where the internal composition of the skeleton becomes important for a proper understanding of the phonological processes involved.

Let us first note some immediate consequences of the Single Melody Theory. A reduplication-specific operation of melody copying is no longer needed, since the skeleton of the reduplicative morpheme can be directly associated with the root melody. But instead of copying, we now apparently need a linearization operation which temporally aligns the reduplicative skeleton with the base skeleton as a prefix, suffix, or infix, and in addition equips it with a duplicate of the parasitized part of the base melody. As it turns out, however, such a reduplication-specific linearization operation is not necessary, since Nonconcatenative Morphology already has a principle which will take care of linearization, namely

Tier Conflation. As introduced and motivated in work by Younes and McCarthy (Younes 1983, McCarthy 1986), Tier Conflation is the non-concatenative version of Bracket Erasure. In Lexical Phonology, Bracket Erasure makes internal morphological structure opaque at certain points of the derivation, the basic idea being that information about morphological structure is not accessible beyond a certain point in the derivation which coincides, according to the standard view, with the end of the level/stratum[4] at which the morphological structure has been created.

A central assumption of Nonconcatenative Morphology, as developed by McCarthy (1979) and in subsequent work, is that morpheme individuation is a geometric property of underlying representations: different morphemes occupy different tiers. In order to make the internal morphological structure of a complex form inaccessible, the different morphemic tiers have to be conflated into a single linearized tier. The way in which Tier Conflation operates is illustrated by the example from Tiberian Hebrew given in (6) (from McCarthy 1986, 226).

---

[4] I will from now on use the terms "level" and "stratum" interchangeably.

(6)
```
        i     e
        |     |      Tier Conflation
      C V C C V C        -->          C V C C V C
      | \ /__/                        | | \ / | |
      s  b                            s i  b  e b
```
                              sibbēb 'he surrounded'

The consonant and vowel tiers of sibbēb 'he surrounded', which express different morphemes, are folded together into a single linearized tier in the process of Tier Conflation. The linear order of the melody elements is determined by the CV skeleton. In order to avoid line crossing, Tier Conflation rewrites multiply linked melody elements when necessary. For the case at hand, the triply linked b melody in (6) cannot survive Tier Conflation in an unmodified form, since the vocalic element e has to intervene. Thus in the output of Tier Conflation the medial CC cluster and the final C slot each have a b melody of their own. Note that Tier Conflation does not transform all multiple linking into melodic sequences of singly linked identicals, which would violate the OCP for all local geminates. The medial geminate b in (6) is not decomposed into two b melodies, since its multiple linking is wellformed even after Tier Conflation.

The empirical arguments for Tier Conflation (cf. Younes 1983, McCarthy 1986) derive from its melody rewriting properties. For example, in Tiberian Hebrew postvocalic stops are spirantized if they are not

geminates. The form in (6) illustrates the effect of this
rule. The medial geminate b is not spirantized, but the
final single b is. The failure of the spirantization rule
to apply to geminates is explainable as geminate blocking,
under any of the several proposed versions of the Geminate
Constraint (Steriade 1982, Steriade and Schein 1984, to
appear, Hayes 1986). Without Tier Conflation and the
concomitant splitting off of the final b element,
Spirantization would not be able to apply to the final
b while leaving the medial geminate b unspirantized.

We can generalize Tier Conflation to the synchronous
skeleta which we encounter in reduplication. In this case
Tier Conflation linearizes CV skeleta and not melody
elements, and the resulting linear order is determined
by the morphological status of the skeleta. In particular,
Tier Conflation makes reference to the prefix/suffix status
of a given reduplicative affix.[5] Equipped with this
information, Tier Conflation linearizes the reduplicative
skeleton next to the root skeleton. I assume that general
principles of locality ensure that linearization takes
place in the immediate neighborhood of the root skeleton
with which the reduplicative skeleton is connected through
the shared melody.

---

[5] I am assuming that infixation can be understood as
prefixation/suffixation plus extraprosodicity, as
persuasively argued by McCarthy and Prince (1985, in
prep.).

Linearization by Tier Conflation is illustrated in (7), using Tagalog initial CV reduplication as an example. Notice that Tier Conflation in this case rewrites the first two melody elements. In this way, Tier Conflation performs the duties of the previously postulated melody copying operation without special stipulations.

(7)
```
        C V
        | |                         TC
        l a k a d        -->        l a l a k a d
        |/\ | | |                   | | |/\ | | |
        C V V C V C                 C V C V V C V C
```

3.1 Rule Overapplication

By assigning the task of linearizing reduplicative skeleta to Tier Conflation, the theory makes predictions about the point(s) in the derivation where linearization occurs. Linearization will take place whenever Tier Conflation/Bracket Erasure is invoked, and at no other time. There has been some discussion in Lexical Phonology about the exact derivational locus of Bracket Erasure (Pesetsky 1979, Mohanan 1981, Kiparsky 1982). I will adopt what I take to be the standard view (Mohanan 1981, Kiparsky 1982), according to which Bracket Erasure is not cyclic, but rather is invoked at the end of each lexical stratum, such that at any given stratum morphological structure created at previous strata is inaccessible. If Tier Conflation/Bracket Erasure is stratal and not cyclic, there is thus a certain delay between morphological formation and morphological destructuring. This delay has an important consequence for reduplicated forms: Until Tier Conflation applies to them, that is, until they exit their stratum of formation, they remain nonlinearized, with synchronous skeleta and doubly linked melody elements. I will argue that overapplication effects appear when phonological rules apply to such representations.

In other words, the whole process of reduplication consists of two derivationally separated components: (i) reduplicative association, i.e. the insertion of the reduplicative template and its association with the base melody, and (ii) reduplicative linearization, i.e. the linearization of the resulting synchronous representation by Tier Conflation at the end of the level. These two components are separated by further morphological and phonological operations, which therefore apply to reduplicated forms in their synchronous representation. In particular, a phonological rule triggered by a costratal affix which is introduced <u>after</u> reduplicative association will apply <u>before</u> reduplicative linearization.

We now have a basis for understanding why rules overapply in reduplication, and the theory also makes predictions as to which rules will overapply.

First, only rules that apply before reduplicative structures are conflated can have overapplication effects. Postlexical rules in particular cannot overapply, since they have no access to nonconflated representations.

Secondly, two distinct properties of the representation are responsible for overapplication effects: (i) the existence of a single, but doubly associated, melody, and (ii) the existence of two simultaneous skeleta.[1] This leads us to distinguish two kinds of overapplication. First, there is what we might call melodic overapplication: Rules which apply to reduplicative structures before Tier Conflation and which affect the doubly associated melody have effects in all of the eventual surface positions of the melody elements. For example, if the melody element p in hypothetical (1) is changed to b following m, b will eventually appear in

---

[1] These two properties are clearly independent, and alternative theories lacking one or the other are imaginable and have in fact been pursued. On the one hand, it is possible to assume simultaneous skeleta without doubly associated melodies, as in Clements 1985, where skeleton is associated to skeleton and the original melody then transferred by another operation. On the other hand, it is also possible to posit doubly associated melodies while keeping sequential skeleta. This possibility (investigated by McCarthy and Prince in unpublished work) arises if the No Crossing Constraint of Autosegmental Phonology is relaxed in certain ways.

two positions after Tier Conflation (tumbalbalik). Melodic overapplication manifests itself in the phonological form of reduplicate and original, but it has no influence on what is copied in reduplication.

(1)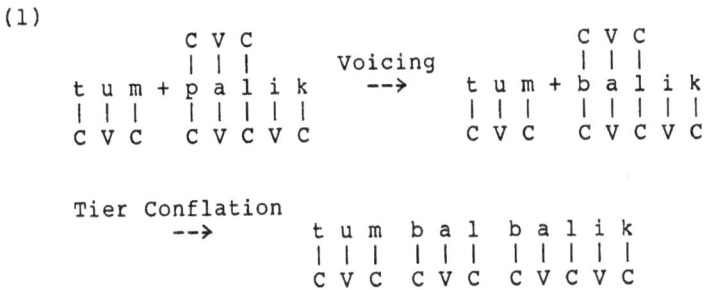

The second type of overapplication might be called skeletal overapplication. I interpret a representation like (1) to mean that both of the simultaneous skeleta are adjacent to the skeleton of the prefix. This seems rather natural: If a is simultaneous with b and b precedes/follows c, then a precedes/follows c. We then expect that both skeleta can be simultaneously affected by certain processes. If for example p is deleted in (1) and the empty onset then filled by resyllabifying m, resyllabification will apply to both the base and the reduplicative skeleton. This becomes particularly clear in the prosodic skeleton theory of McCarthy and Prince (1985, in prep.), where (1) appears as something like (2), with the reduplicative template specified as a single syllable.

(2)
```
              σ                              σ
             /|\         Deletion           |\
    t u m + p a l i k      -->     t u m + ∅ a l i k
    \|/   \|  \|/                   \|/     |  \|/
     σ     σ   σ                     σ      σ   σ

                         σ
    Resyll.             .'|\         TC
     -->      t u m·    a l i k      -->    t u m a l m a l i k
              \|≠  '.   |  \|/                \|/ \|/   \|  \|/
               σ    ·σ   σ                     σ   σ    σ   σ
```

Deleting the melody element p in (2) leaves two onsetless syllables; resyllabifying m amounts to associating m to both of the simultaneous syllables, and the form appears as tumalmalik after Tier Conflation, where the reduplicated m originated in a morpheme outside of the morphological domain of reduplication. Skeletal overapplication thus shows itself in what is copied in reduplication, it is in a sense "overcopying".

Let us then return to Tagalog Nasal Substitution, the classical case of overapplication mentioned in the preceding section. To briefly recapitulate, this rule replaces root-initial obstruents by their homorganic nasals after certain prefixes ending in a nasal. Reduplicative overapplication of Nasal Substitution is evidenced by the gerunds in (3). For example, the root pulah 'red' has the corresponding gerund pa-mu-mulah, formed by initial CV reduplication and prefixation of the nasal-substituting prefix paN.

(3)
pulah	pa-mu-mulah	'turning red'
ta:kot	pa-na-na:kot	'frightening'
ka?ilaŋan	pa-ŋa-ŋa?ilaŋan	'needing'

We will assume that the prefix-final nasal elements which trigger Nasal Substitution are underlyingly unspecified for place. Nasal Substitution is a melody-plane rule spreading the nasal feature onto the melodic core of a following consonant. We can now understand the overapplication of Nasal Substitution as arising in the way indicated in (4).

(4) a. Reduplication
     and Affixation
     of paN:
```
                C V
                | |
         p a N+ t a k o t
                |/\ | | |
                C V V C V C
```

  b. Nasal
     Substitution:
```
                C V
                | |
         p a  n a k o t
                |/\ | | |
                C V V C V C
```

  c. Tier
     Conflation:
```
         p a n a n   a k o t
         | | | | |  /\ | | |
         C V C V C V V C V C
```
     panana:kot 'frightening'

The reduplicative CV affix enters the representation on a tier of its own and is associated left-to-right with the root melody; then paN is prefixed to the result (4a). Before Tier Conflation, Nasal Substitution applies to this representation, changing t into n (4b). Finally, at the point when Tier Conflation linearizes this representation, part of the melody has to be rewritten in order to avoid line crossing; this holds in particular for the multiply linked n derived by Nasal Substitution, which is in this way placed into its two surface positions (4c).

For this derivation to be possible, Nasal Substitution must have a chance to apply before the representation is irrevocably flattened by Tier Conflation, that is, Nasal Substitution and reduplication must be costratal. In particular, Nasal Substitution cannot be a postlexical rule. The lexical status of Nasal Substitution is independently confirmed by the fact that the rule is triggered only by a highly specific class of nasal-final prefixes and furthermore has a number of exceptions (see Carrier 1979, 54-79).

Note that the the Tagalog case of overapplication cannot be characterized as just involving the application of a phonological rule (Nasal Substitution) before a morphological operation (reduplication). Such interactions are a systematic feature of Lexical Phonology, provided the phonological rule in question is triggered by earlier morphology. What is not possible in Lexical Phonology, however, is for a phonological rule triggered by _later_ morphology to precede reduplication. But this is exactly what would have to be stipulated for the Tagalog overapplication case, where the prefix _paN_, which triggers Nasal Substitution, is manifestly attached _after_ reduplication. Note that well-motivated principles of word formation prohibit an inversion of the order of the two morphological operations. Such a derivation would proceed as follows: First the prefix _paN_ is attached to the unreduplicated root, then Nasal Substitution applies to the result, and finally the reduplicative affix is inserted _between_ prefix and root. This would only be possible in an unconstrained theory of morphology which freely permits violations of morphological locality, such that after affixing _a_ to _b_ another morpheme _c_ can be inserted between _a_ and _b_. In the absence of evidence for a theory of morphology with such power it appears imperative to maintain the principle of morphological locality, which entails that the derivation just sketched is impossible.

3.1.1 Dakota

There is a substantial number of phonological rules in various languages which overapply in reduplicative constructions. An interesting example appears in Dakota (Siouan, Mississippi Valley) and is discussed in Shaw (1976) (all examples cited below are drawn from this work). Dakota has a rule of Velar Palatalization by which the voiceless velar stops (plain, glottalized, and aspirated k) are fronted to their corresponding palatals after the front vowels i and e, as indicated in (5).

(5)
$$\begin{bmatrix} k \\ k^? \\ k^h \end{bmatrix} \longrightarrow \begin{bmatrix} \check{x} \\ \check{c}^? \\ \check{x}^h \end{bmatrix} / \{^i_e\} \underline{\quad}$$ (under complex morphological conditions)

Following Cowper and Rice (1985), the rule is stated in (6) as a purely melodic operation spreading [-back] from e and i onto the melodic core (identified by its [+cons] specification) of a following velar, delinking the feature [+back].

(6)   [-back]   [+back]
         | ·.   ǂ
         | ·.
       [-cons]   [+cons]

Velar Palatalization is clearly lexical and applies under complex morphological conditions, see Shaw (1976) for a detailed investigation. The forms in (7) show alternations due to Velar Palatalization. The stem k^hute 'to shoot at' appears with a velar after the first person object prefix ma (ma-k^hute) but with a palatal after the second person object prefix ni (ni-$č^h$ute). The stem kahíta 'sweep' alternates in a parallel manner.

(7)   ma-k^húte   ni-$č^h$úte
          'he shoots at me'   'he shoots at you'
       wa-káhita   i-čáhite
          'I sweep'   'broom' (instr.+sweep)

Dakota reduplication, which expresses a number of morphological categories (plural, repetition, distributive, and intensive), is analyzed in Marantz (1982) as final CCVC reduplication. Some examples are given in (8) (the effects of a later epenthesis rule applying to consonant-final stems have been suppressed for clarity).

(8)
   h̃aska   h̃aska-ska   'tall'
   apʰa   apʰa -pʰa   'to hit'
   tʰũk   tʰũk -tʰũk-   'to hesitate'
   xap   xap -xap-   'to rustle'

The forms in (9a,b) illustrate overapplication of Velar Palatalization in reduplicated forms. Note that the devoicing of obstruents in syllable-final position evidenced by the surface forms given in (9) is due to a postlexical (and therefore post-conflational) rule.

(9)
 a. kaǵ ki-čaǵ-čaǵ- 'to make'
  e.g. wičʰa-ki-čax-čax-ʔiyeya
    'he made it for them quickly'
 b. koz ki-čoz-čoz- 'to wave'
  e.g. nape ki-čos-čoz-a
    'he waved his hand to him'

The root <u>kaǵ</u> is reduplicated as <u>čaǵ-čaǵ</u> after the prefix <u>ki</u>, where both occurrences of the root-inital consonant show the effects of Palatalization. Similarly <u>koz</u> 'to wave'in (9b) is reduplicated as <u>čoz-čoz</u>, where again both occurrences of the root-initial consonant are palatalized. The derivation of the first form is given in (10).

(10) a. Reduplication and Prefixation

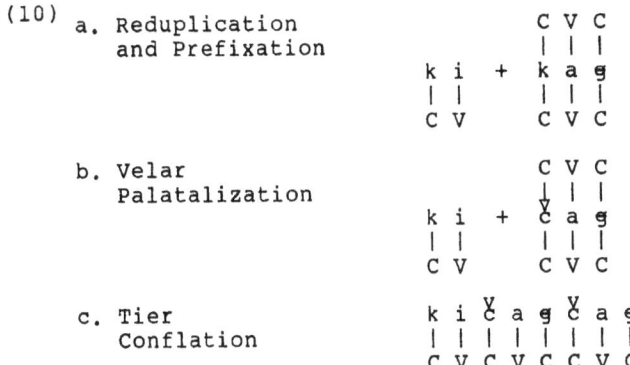

b. Velar Palatalization

c. Tier Conflation

After reduplication and prefixation of ki- (10a), Velar Palatalization, as a lexical rule, applies to the non-linearized structure and palatalizes the shared melody element k after i (10b). Subsequently Tier Conflation rewrites the resulting palatal and produces the two surface occurrences of the element (10c).[2]

---

[2]Shaw (1976), working in a framework with linear rule application, argues that the overapplication of Velar Palatalization cannot be explained by letting the rule apply to the unreduplicated form and then reduplicating the result. She points out that this order of application leads to an ordering paradox when other rules of Dakota phonology (Epenthesis and Ablaut) are taken into account. It is not clear, however, whether the ordering paradox argument still holds in Lexical Phonology, and an alternative derivation cannot be ruled out in which prefixation of ki- takes place first (ki+kaǧ), Velar Palatalization applies to the result and derives ki+čaǧ, and the last syllable is then reduplicated rightwards as ki+čaǧ-čaǧ.

3.1.2 Sanskrit

An instructive example of overapplication is presented by the Sanskrit <u>ruki</u> rule which retroflexes s to ṣ after r, after velar stops, and after the high vowels i and u. As amply demonstrated by Kiparsky (1982), the <u>ruki</u> rule is lexical and applies regularly to inflectional and derivational endings and also (with lexical exceptions) to noninitial members of compounds and to clitics. The <u>ruki</u> cases which are of interest here are found in combinations of verbal prefixes with verbs: If the prefix ends in a <u>ruki</u>-trigger (e.g. <u>ab^{h}i</u> 'to', <u>prati</u> 'against', <u>vi</u> 'apart', <u>ni</u> 'down, into'), the rule applies to an initial s of the verb root, as illustrated by the forms in (11) (from Whitney 1889, 63). Whitney remarks that "such combinations are both of great frequency and of peculiar intimacy, analogous with those of root or stem and affix [...]; the cases are numberless."

(11)
    sañj   'hang'   abʰi-sañj
    sac   'accompany'   abʰi-ṣac
    stʰā   'stand'   prati-ṣṭʰā
    sā, si   'bind'   ví-ṣita
    sic   'pour out'   ní-ṣikta

As illustrated in (12), perfect forms of verbs are formed by reduplicating the initial CV sequence of the root. If the root begins with a consonant cluster, the first consonant is reduplicated, except for s̲ + obstruent clusters, which instead reduplicate the obstruent following the s̲.

(12)
    sañj   'hang'   sa-sañj
    druh   'hurt'   du-druh
    spand   'quiver'   pa-spand

We find overapplication of ruki when a prefix ending in a ruki-trigger combines with a reduplicated verb. An example is the perfect form in (13) (cited after Kiparsky 1982, 77). Note that the second ṣ in (13) is clearly not in a ruki-environment in the surface form.

(13)   abʰi-ṣa-ṣañja   'cursed'   sañj   'hang'

The formulation of the ruki rule in terms of
distinctive features has always presented something of
a problem, I will here follow Kiparsky (1982, 75) in
assuming that retroflex consonants are characterized by
the feature combination [+coronal, +high, +back] and that
[+high] uniquely characterizes the class of ruki triggers.
The rule is stated in (14) as spreading [+high] onto an
adjacent coronal fricative, simultaneously adding the
specification [+back]. The exact formulation is of little
interest in the present context, the only important point
being the rather obvious one that the rule can be stated
in strictly melodic terms.

(14)
$$\begin{array}{cc} [+\text{high}] & [+\text{back}] \\ | & \vdots \\ & [+\text{cor}] \\ | & | \\ [\ldots] & \left[\begin{array}{c} +\text{cont} \\ -\text{son} \end{array}\right] \end{array}$$

As indicated in (15), the overapplication of ruki
in reduplicated forms like (13) is readily accounted for
if the rule has a chance to apply to reduplicative
representations before Tier Conflation (for typographical
reasons I have left out the [+back] specification
introduced by (14)).

(15)
```
            [+high] C V
               |˙.  | |
            a bʰi +˙s a ñ j a        _
            | | |   | | | |        abʰi-sa-sanja
            V C V   C V C V            ˙  ˙
```

Preconflational application of <u>ruki</u> to combinations of prefixes with reduplicated verbs is found in a second class of cases, namely in forms where a root-initial <u>s</u> is skipped in reduplication and therefore does not end up surface-adjacent to the prefix, but nevertheless exhibits <u>ruki</u> effects. As indicated above, this situation arises in roots with initial <u>s</u>+obstruent clusters, which in Sanskrit reduplicate the obstruent instead of the <u>s</u>. Thus <u>sthā</u> 'to stand' in (16a) is reduplicated as <u>ta-sthā</u> (with deaspiration of the reduplicated consonant by Grassmann's Law, as discussed below in section 3.3). When such forms are combined with <u>ruki</u>-triggering prefixes, the rule again "overapplies", here in the sense that it apparently applies across the intervening reduplication, as can be seen in (16b).

(16)
    a.   sthā 'to stand'   ta-sthā
    b.   vi-ta-sṭhe
                                                    vi-ta-sṭhire
                                                    abhi-ta-sṭhan

Essentially following Steriade's (1982) analysis, we can ascribe the special behavior of s̱+obstruent clusters in Sanskrit to a restriction on association to the effect that only syllabified melodic material is eligible for association with the reduplicative template. Under the assumption that s̱ in an initial s̱+obstruent cluster is still extrasyllabic when reduplication takes place, the forms in (16) can be derived as in (17).

(17)
```
                 C V
     [+high]     | |
        \   .    | |
      v i +·s  t^h a
      | |    | | |
      C V    C C V
              \ |
               ṣ       vi-ta-sṭʰa
```

When the reduplicative template is associated with the root melody, the unsyllabified s̱ has to be skipped because of the special restriction on association. Subsequent prefixation of vi creates the ruki context, and the rule applies in the melody plane of the unconflated representation. Finally Tier Conflation intercalates the reduplicated sequence ta between i and s̱.

The forms in (17b) are instructive in a second respect: Note that the assimilation of t^h to the preceding retroflex ṣ is not transmitted when the consonant is reduplicated (vi-ta-ṣṭha, not *vi-ta-ṣṭha).³ This assimilation process therefore has to follow Tier Conflation, which fits well which its exceptionless character (cf. Whitney 1889, 67: "A dental surd mute or nasal, or the dental sibilant, when immediately preceded by a ṣ, is everywhere converted into the corresponding lingual.")

The strictly melodic statement of the <u>ruki</u> rule given above in (14) explains another apparent violation of locality which occurs in prefix-verb combinations: the rule applies across an intervening augment a, as in (18).

(18)
    abhy-a-sthām   pary-a-sasvajat   vy-a-sahanta
    ny-a-sadāma   abhy-a-siñcan   vy-a-stabhāt

Let us hypothesize that the augment is a totally featureless vowel (i.e. a V slot without an associated melodic core) which is later spelled out as the default vowel a. The <u>ruki</u> rule can then apply across such a vowel

---

³Underlying retroflex stops are rare in rootinitial position, but where they occur they preserve their retroflexion in reduplication:

(i)   ṭank   'cover'   ṭaṭanka (pres.)
        ḍī   'fly'   didye (perf.), adīdayat (aor.)
        dhauk   'approach'   dudhauke (perf.)

slot since, as a strictly melodic rule, it demands only core-adjacency, not skeleton-adjacency.[4]

Returning to reduplicated forms, it is worth noting that the ruki rule interacts in a second and quite different way with reduplication, due to the fact that it applies not only before, but also after Tier Conflation. In its postconflational applications, ruki retroflexes the second occurrence of rootinitial s in reduplicated forms, as shown in (19).

(19)   si-ṣyade   su-ṣvāpa   si-ṣāsati

Here ruki applies between the reduplicative parts, and this can only happen after Tier Conflation. Since at this point Tier Conflation has already split the reduplicated melody element s into two separate occurrences, there is no overapplication effect, and only the occurrence of s which actually stands in the ruki environment appears with retroflexion.

---

[4]I am assuming that the lack of a melodic core is a specific property of the augment and does not hold for a in general, otherwise we would expect the ruki rule always to apply across a, which is contrary to the facts.

3.1.3 Madurese

The overapplying rules considered in the preceding two sections (Dakota Palatalization and Sanskrit <u>ruki</u>) both involved local segmental operations in the melody plane. I will now show that harmony processes can overapply in reduplicative structures in the same way.

A case of this kind is found in Madurese, a Western Austronesian language spoken on the island of Madura and on a small part of Java (Stevens 1968, 1985, Hirschbühler 1978). Madurese has a rule of Nasal Harmony which propagates Nasalization rightwards from nasal consonants through glottals (h,?) and glides. Nasal Harmony is blocked by other consonants. The operation of the rule is illustrated by the forms in (20).

(20)

nãse?	'rice'
o-mãtao	'to pretend to know'
mãõs	'to read'
e-nãẽ?ẽ	'be climbed on'
mãhã	'great'
nẽỹãt	'intention'
mõw̃ã	'face'

Madurese has several kinds of reduplication (see Weeda 1986 for a recent thorough investigation). The kind of reduplication which is of interest here (called "End

Reduplication" in Stevens 1968) serves to indicate plurality, frequency of action, and nondirected action, among other things. It can informally be described as copying the final syllable of the word at the beginning. Some examples are given in (21).

(21)
    abit   bit-abit   'finally'
    buwa?   wa?-buwa?   'fruits'

Marantz (1982, 451) analyzed this as initial CVC prefixation with marked linking between melody and the prefixed reduplicative template, i.e. right-to-left instead of left-to-right, and I will here adopt this assumption.[5]

The interesting point in the present context is the fact that Nasal Harmony overapplies in reduplicated forms, as shown in (22).

(22) ẽn-mãẽn   'toys'
      wã-mõwã   'faces'
      yat-nẽyãt   'intentions'

The nasalization appearing in the reduplicated part of these forms cannot be accounted for if Nasal Harmony

---

[5] It has been pointed out by Broselow and McCarthy (1984) and also by McCarthy and Prince in unpublished work that the status of the marked linking option in reduplication is somewhat dubious. Only very few cases are known where marked linking has to be invoked, and most of them are amenable to other analyses. Madurese End Reduplication appears to be related to a kind of compounding in which the first compound member is truncated to its last syllable, as illustrated in (i).

(i) sar-suri   pasar   suri
     'afternoon market'   'market'   'afternoon'

     riŋ-tua   uriŋ   tua
     'parents'   'person'   'old'

Radical truncation of this kind is certainly unusual among the world's languages. In Madurese it leads in a number of cases to opacity (see Stevens 1968, 102), and it is rather doubtful whether it can count as a productive synchronic process. If it is a productive process, and if end-reduplicated forms are derived by total reduplication followed by radical truncation, the overapplication of Nasal Harmony in end-reduplicated forms discussed below can alternatively be accounted for by applying Nasal Harmony independently in both parts of the reduplicated form before truncation.

operates on a linearized representation, since the rule
spreads nasality exclusively to the right and is always
blocked by obstruents. The last form in (22) constitutes
crucial evidence in the present context: While there might
be some doubt whether nasalized and nonnasalized vowels
are clearly distinguishable before syllable-final nasals,
there is no way in which the nasalization of the
reduplicated a in the last form could be ascribed to some
local nasalization process. We can explain the
overapplication of Nasal Harmony in Madurese if we assume
that the rule operates in the melody plane, as indicated
in (23), and precedes Tier Conflation. Subsequent Tier
Conflation rewrites some of the nasal autosegments, as
also indicated in (23).

(23)
```
               C V C
               | | |
         +N    | | |    -N
          |∙∙∙.| | | /
          |  ∙∙∙.| |/           TC      +N -N  +N     -N
          n e y a t              -->    /| /   /|\ \   |
          | | | | |                     y a t  n e y a t
          C V C V C                     | | |  | | | | |
                                        C V C  C V C V C
```

3.1.4 Chumash

We have so far discussed cases of melodic
overapplication where strictly melodic rules apply to
shared melodies, with the result that elements outside

of the domain of reduplication caused changes in both parts
of a reduplicated form. In a second class of cases,
overapplication of rules has an influence on how much of
a form appears copied after Tier Conflation in reduplicated
forms: It looks as if phonology redraws the boundaries
of the material to be reduplicated and induces
"overcopying". Besides the shared melody, such examples
directly involve the two simultaneous skeleta of a
reduplicative structure.

As a representative example for this type of
overapplication, I will here discuss initial CVC
reduplication in Ineseño Chumash, a language once spoken
in Southern California. The following analysis is based
on the work of Applegate (1976), where all Chumash forms
cited below are to be found.

Chumash uses stem-initial CVC reduplication both
lexically and in order to mark plurals, distributives,
intensives etc. Some examples appear in (24). As
illustrated in (24b), prefixal material is not
reduplicated, but rather appears outside the reduplicated
portion of the word.[6]

---

[6] In these examples, s- is the third person subject prefix;
alternations between s and š are due to long-distance
sibilant harmony and to a local dissimilation rule
palatalizing s before nonstrident coronals, see Poser
(1982) for a detailed analysis; a general process applying
to reduplicated nouns is responsible for the additional
final glottalization appearing in some of the examples.

(24) a. čʰumaš   čʰum-čʰumaš?   'islanders, Chumash people'
       pon   pon-pon?   'trees'
       t?aya   t?ay-t?aya?   'abalones'
    b. s + čeq   š + čeq-čeq   'it is very torn'
       s + kitwon   s + kit-kitwon   'it is coming out'
       s + tipʰɨn   š + tip-tipʰɨn   'it is heavily forested'

There are, however, several systematic exceptions to the generalization that prefixal material is not reduplicated. Applegate (1976, 279) remarks that "[w]ith vowel-initial stems, the reduplicated sequence maintains an invariant CVC shape by including any consonant immediately preceding the stem". Consider the following examples (k- 1st pers., s- 3rd pers., iš- dual, iy- plural):

(25) k + ic?is   kic-kic?is?   'my sisters'
     s + ikuk   sik-sikuk   'he is chopping'
     s + iš + expeč   ši + šex-šexpeč   'they two are singing'
     s + iy + eqwel   si + yeq-yeqel   'they are making'

The "overcopying" of prefixal material that we find in (25) can be formally understood as the overapplication of onset formation in reduplicative structures. I will

here depart from my usual expository practice and adopt
a prosodic skeleton in the sense of McCarthy and Prince
(1985, in prep.), since this greatly facilitates the
analysis. Let us assume that the reduplicative template
is specified as "syllable", with the understanding that
a template expands maximally in association (in this case,
into a heavy syllable) unless it carries a specific
restriction (e.g. to monomoraicity). The overcopying
phenomenon evidenced in (25) can then be understood as
indicated in (26), where prefixal s is incorporated into
two simultaneous syllables which both lack an onset.

(26)
```
     .σ
   . Ⅰ\
s.+i k u k   -->    s i k s i k u k
 ·.Ⅰ \Ⅰ/            \Ⅰ/ \Ⅰ \Ⅰ/
    σ  σ             σ   σ   σ
```

Overcopying of prefixal material occurs not only with
vowel-initial stems but also with stems beginning with
a glottal stop. When such stems are reduplicated, the
glottal stop coalesces with an immediately preceding
prefixal consonant into a single glottalized segment, and

the entire glottalized consonant is reduplicated. This is shown by the forms in (27).[7]

(27)

k + ʔanis	kʔan-kʔanis	'my parental uncles'
p + ʔayakuyʔ	pʔay-pʔayakuyʔ	'your basket'
s + ʔaminʔ	sʔam-sʔaminʔ	'he is naked'

Glottal Coalescence is formulated in (28), where a glottal stop spreads its laryngeal features to a preceding consonantal core and loses its own melodic core. Since place of articulation features are lacking in a glottal stop, the glottalization of the preceding consonant is its only relic.

---

[7]The same phenomenon is observed in stems with initial /h/, where /h/ coalesces with a preceding obstruent into a single aspirate which is reduplicated intact, as shown in (i). Different from the cases with initial glottal stop, however, the coalescence of /h/ with preceding obstruents is optional, and reduplicated forms can occur with or without overcopying of the preceding obstruent, apparently in free variation.

(i) k + hawaʔ   kʰaw-kʰawaʔ, kʰaw-hawaʔ
                    'my maternal uncles'

Because of the variability of the cases with initial /h/, I will limit my discussion to the stems with initial /ʔ/.

(28) Glottal Coalescence

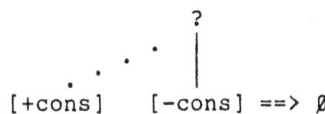

[+cons]   [-cons] ==> ∅

The application of Glottal Coalescence is illustrated in (29). The syllabic affiliations are suppressed here and the melodic core is expressed by small cv's to distinguish them from the skeleton.

(29)
```
                        Glottal
                        Coalescence
Laryngeal:       ʔ      =========>        ʔ
                  \                      . ⤲
Melodic Core:  c +  c v c v c         c + ∅ v c v c
                \    \ \ \ \           \    \ \ \ \
Place:         k      a n i s         k      a n i s
```

The derivation of kʔan-kʔanis 'my parental uncles' is shown in (30).

(30) a. Reduplication
        and Prefixation
```
                         σ
                        /|\
                    k + ʔ a n i s
                     \|   \|/
                     σ    σ
```

b. Glottal
   Coalescence
```
                         σ
                        |\
                    kʔ  ∅ a n i s    (see (29))
                     |    \|/
                     σ    σ
```

        c. Onset   σ
           Formation   . ⋅ |\
                             k ʔ   a n i s
                               ⋅. | \|/
                                  σ   σ

        d. Tier   kʔa n kʔa n i s
           Conflation   \|/ \| \|/
                                   σ   σ   σ

Glottal Coalescence results in the loss of the onset for the initial syllable (30b), and Onset Formation applies as in the vowel-initial cases (30c). After Tier Conflation, the glottalized consonant appears both in the stem and in the reduplication (30d).

The derivation in (30) crucially assumes that Glottal Coalescence (28) takes place before Tier Conflation. This receives independent support in Applegate's (1976, 280) observation that the sequence <u>consonant + glottal stop</u> does not always coalesce into a single glottalized segment. For example, the melodic sequence /mʔ/ in (31), which is created through reduplication, arises only after Tier Conflation.

(31)   ʔemet   ʔem-ʔemet ʔ   'ground squirrels'

Applegate points out that the sequence /mʔ/ in (31) is realized as [Mʔ], i.e. as a voiceless nasal followed by a glottal stop, and contrasts with the glottalized sonorant

/m$^?$/ (phonetically [?m], with the glottal closure preceding the sonorant). This is consistent with and supports our hypothesis that Glottal Coalescence is lexical and applies before Tier Conflation, as in (30).

3.1.5 Kihehe

Overcopying phenomena amenable to the same basic analysis occur in Kihehe (a Bantu language of Tanzania). Odden and Odden (1985), working in Marantz's (1982) framework, describe and analyse Kihehe reduplication as a case where several phonological rules have to precede melody copying. Reduplication in Kihehe is stem reduplication, more exactly, leftward reduplication of the root plus following extensions and suffixes. Prefixes are not reduplicated, but attached at the left margin of the reduplicated form. This is shown by the examples in (32) (all examples are taken from Odden and Odden 1985; the acute mark indicates high tones, low tones are unmarked).

(32) kú-haáta   kú-haata-haáta
    'to ferment'   'to start fermenting'

    mi-dóodo   mi-doodo-dóodo
    'little'   'fairly little'

    kú-gula   kú-fi-gula-gúla
    'to buy'   'to buy a bit of them'

In (32) the general reduplication procedure is illustrated for consonant-initial verb roots. Vowel-initial roots show interestingly different behavior, as illustrated in (33).

(33) stem <u>ita</u> 'pour'
    ku-ita --> kwíita   kwíita-kwíita
           'to pour'   'to pour a bit'

    ku-lu-ita --> kú-lwiíta   kú-lwiita-lwiíta
              'to pour it'   'to pour it a bit'

In the case of a stem like <u>ita</u> 'pour' in (33), a rule gliding short high vowels in prevocalic position applies to the infinitival form <u>ku</u> + <u>ita</u> to derive (with compensatory lengthening and resyllabification) <u>kwiita</u>. The corresponding reduplication is not *<u>kwiita-ita</u>, but <u>kwiita-kwiita</u>. Prefixal material is copied, because it is phonologically integrated into the stem.

We can understand the gliding of high vowels as taking place in two steps. First, prevocalic high vowels, together with a preceding consonant, are syllabified in prevocalic position as the first mora of a bimoraic syllable. In the case of the simple form kwiita, this takes place as follows:

(34)

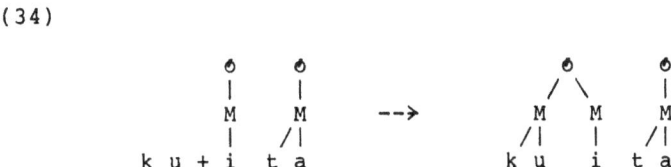

Demoraification of the high vowel (and the concomitant compensatory lengthening) is the result of a rule which associates a following vowel with the mora node dominating the high vowel, as formulated in (35).

(35)

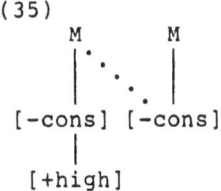

Rule (35) changes (34) into (36), where the melody i is linked to two moras.

(36)

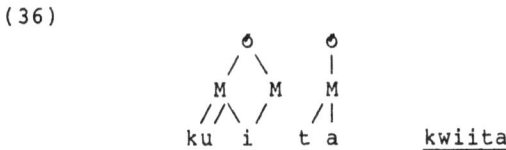

In reduplicated forms the same processes apply, only this time in both dimensions of the simultaneous representation. The derivation of kwiita-kwiita is shown in (37).

(37)
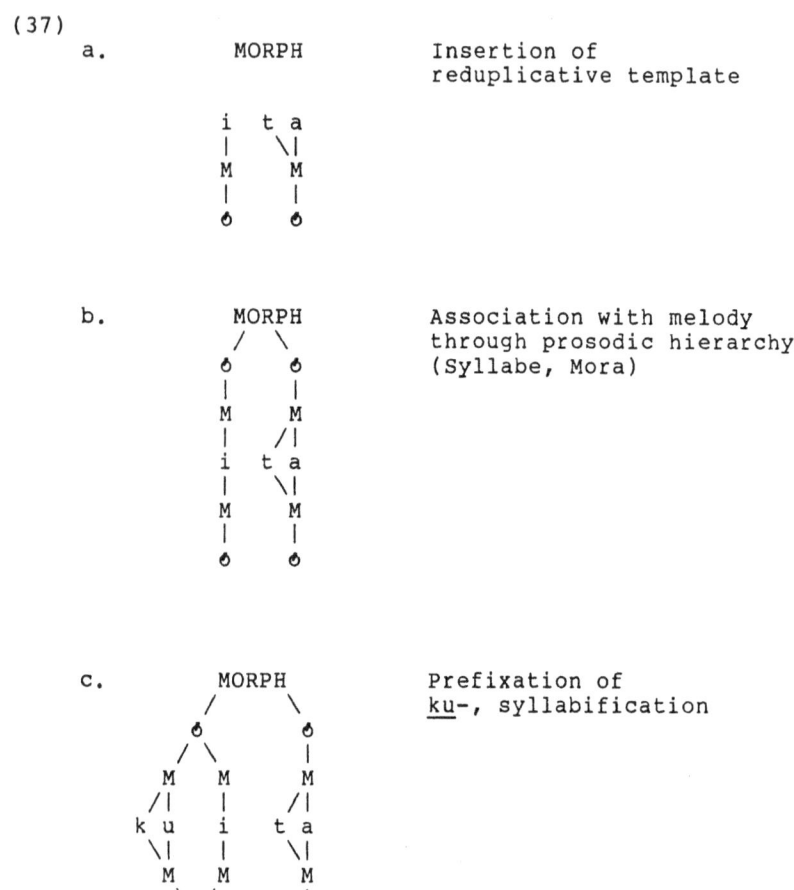

a. MORPH — Insertion of reduplicative template

b. MORPH — Association with melody through prosodic hierarchy (Syllabe, Mora)

c. MORPH — Prefixation of ku-, syllabification

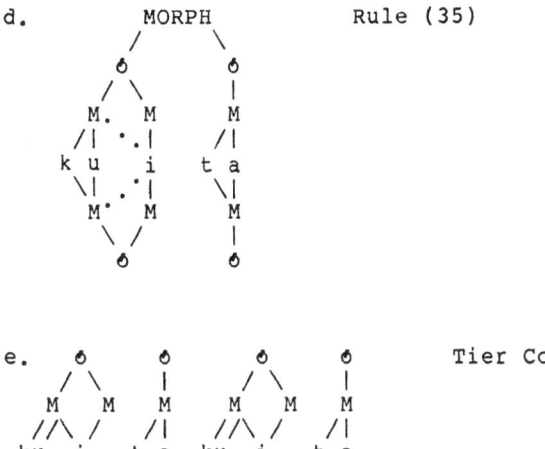

d. MORPH   Rule (35)

e. Tier Conflation

kwiitakwiita

Following Odden and Odden (1985), I assume that the reduplicative template is specified as 'morpheme' (abbreviated as "MORPH", to keep it distinct from "mora" (= M)). The melody of the domain over which the reduplication is defined then gets associated (37b). Melody elements cannot be directly connected to a node like 'morpheme', they communicate with the template through the prosodic hierarchy (in this case, minimally through the constituents mora and syllable). In (37c), the prefix ku- is added and syllabified. This takes place before

Tier Conflation,[8] therefore the high vowel u and the preceding k are integrated into the two simultaneous syllable nodes associated with the following vowel melody i. To this representation applies rule (35), demoraifying u and lengthening i (37d). Finally Tier Conflation rewrites the melodic material associated with the simultaneous prosodic constituents and derives (37e).[9]

---

[8]Lisa Selkirk has pointed out that there are reasons to attach prefixes in Kihehe at a later lexical level than suffixes (arguments to this effect can be found in recent work by Scott Myers on the Bantu language Shona). This creates a problem for the assumption that Tier Conflation has not yet applied at the point when the prefix ku- is added, given our hypothesis that Tier Conflation takes place at the end of a lexical level. I leave this as a problem for further investigation.

[9]Odden and Odden (1985) show that two other rules in Kihehe - Glide Epenthesis and Nasal Adjunction - overapply in reduplicated forms in a similar way but with further complications. As pointed out by Schlindwein (1986), Nasal Adjunction in Kihehe is a complex process with both lexical and postlexical components, which leads to surface complications in the compensatory lengthening of preceding vowels. In certain morphological contexts voiceless stops are replaced by a preceding nasal, whereas voiced stops and sonorants form complex segments. The correct distribution of vowel length can be derived if replacement takes place lexically but complex segment formation only postlexically (= post-conflationally, for our purposes). This is not an unreasonable assumption, and following Schlindwein (1986) we can derive the distinction from Structure Preservation if we assume that nasal contour segments are not underlying and hence cannot be created during the lexical phonology.

This concludes our treatment of rule overapplication in reduplicative constructions. We have seen that the Single Melody Theory of reduplication, which regards reduplicative morphemes as skeletal templates simultaneous with the root skeleton and directly associated with the root melody, can explain overapplication of phonological rules in a natural way. Overapplication effects appear whenever lexical rules apply after insertion and association of the reduplicative template but before Tier Conflation and affect the shared melody or the two simultaneous skeleta. We have analyzed Dakota Velar Palatalization (section 3.1.1), Sanskrit <u>ruki</u> (section 3.1.2), and Madurese Nasal Harmony (section 3.1.3) as melodic rules applying to the single but shared melody, thereby explaining the changes in both parts of reduplicated forms. The overcopying effects of Chumash Glottal Coalescence (section 3.1.4) and Kihehe Glide Formation (section 3.1.5) have been shown to result from prosodic reorganizations affecting both of the simultaneous skeleta of a reduplicative representation.

3.2 Rule Underapplication

Unexpected interactions of reduplication with phonological rules are not restricted to overapplication; there is also the negative counterpart, underapplication, where a rule does not apply in a reduplicative construction even though its context is apparently met in one part. Rule underapplication is somewhat less frequent than rule overapplication (or has less frequently been taken note of), but a number of clear cases have appeared in the literature. In terms of the theory developed here, underapplication effects arise in the following situation: At the level where reduplication takes place, the structural description of a certain rule is not met in the synchronous representation of reduplicated forms, so the rule does not apply; its structural description is met after Tier Conflation, which is however too late for the rule to have a chance to apply.

Two kinds of underapplication can be distinguished. The first is quite straightforward and arises when one part of a reduplicated form would have to provide the context for a rule applying in the other part. In this case the structural description of the rule is not met before Tier Conflation because elements which have to be adjacent for the rule to apply only come into adjacency through Tier Conflation. As a simple illustration, consider the following case. Sapir (1930, 49) reports for Southern Paiute that "[w]hen an initial w comes, by derivation or compounding, to stand after a vowel, it regularly becomes nasalized to -ŋw-". Illustrative examples are given in (1).

(1)

    wa'ani-   'to shout'
    tiŋwa'ani-   'to give a good shout'

    winɛ-   'to stand'
    yaŋwɛŋwinɛxa' 'while standing and holding'

Sapir states that there is one systematic exception: "This rule does not operate, however, when w becomes intervocalic by reduplication." Consider the reduplicated forms in (2), where w in derived intervocalic position is not replaced by ŋw:

(2)

    wigi-   'vulva'
    wiwixiA   'vulvas'

    wagi-   'several enter'
    wawaxxIpiga' 'all entered'

This is the expected result if the relevant rule is applicable only before Tier Conflation. As shown in (3), the segment w is not yet in an intervocalic environment.

(3)

       'vulvas'

The second kind of underapplication is closely linked to a specific representational property of the present approach, namely to the fact that before Tier Conflation reduplicative constructions possess doubly associated melody elements. If we take these multiple associations seriously and think of the melody elements involved as "nonlinear" geminates, we can expect them to share certain properties with linear geminates.

(4)
   a. linear geminates   b. nonlinear geminates

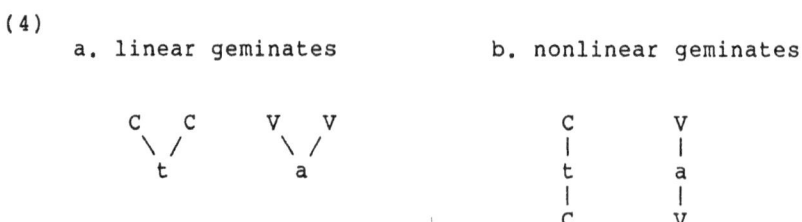

In particular, the Geminate Constraint (Kenstowicz and Pyle 1973, Guerssel 1978, Steriade 1982, Hayes 1986, Steriade and Schein 1984, to appear) might be expected to govern both linear and nonlinear geminates. We will see below in section 3.2.2 that there are indeed cases of rule underapplication whose explanation crucially involves an appeal to the Geminate Constraint. This second kind of rule underapplication is more indirect than the first since it involves an abstract principle of Phonological Theory, and it is interesting in the present context because it lends support to the hypothesis that reduplication is characterized by shared melodies.

3.2.1 Missing linear context

Let us now turn to the first type of underapplication and examine it in greater detail. We will consider two cases where a phonological rule underapplies because its linear context is not present inside reduplicative structures. We have already seen how this can come about: Certain melody elements stand in derived adjacency after but not before Tier Conflation, so a preconflational rule requiring their adjacency will not be able to apply.

3.2.1.1 Chumash

A first case of this kind appears in Chumash. According to Applegate (1976), Chumash has a general rule of l-Deletion deleting l before dental segments (5).

(5)   l-Deletion

   l ==> ∅ / __ [+cor]

The rule of l-deletion (5) is illustrated in (6). The final l of the prefix pil- 'through the air' deletes before t in (6a) but is preserved before k in (6b).

(6)
   a. /s-pil-tap/   -->   spitap   'it falls in'
   b. /s-pil-kowon/   -->   spilkowon   'it spills'

Chumash has a productive process of stem-initial CVC reduplication which we discussed in section 3.1.4 above as a case of overapplication. The same reduplicative process also shows examples of rule underapplication. Applegate (1976, 281) points out that l-Deletion (5) underapplies in reduplicated forms whenever the target l forms the end of the reduplicated portion and the contextual coronal occurs at the beginning of the original stem, witness the forms in (7).

(7)
   (š +)ta<u>l</u>-<u>t</u>al[?]ik[?] 'his wives (of a chief)'
    c[?]a<u>l</u>-<u>c</u>[?]aluqay[?] 'cradles'
  (?aya +)tu<u>l</u>-<u>t</u>ulutul[?] 'butterflies'

This is the expected result if <u>l</u>-Deletion applies to reduplicative structures before Tier Conflation - at this stage of the derivation, <u>l</u> is obviously not adjacent to the root-initial coronal, as illustrated by the representation in (8) for the second example in (7).

(8)
```
        C V C
        | | |
        c?a l u q a y?
        | | | | | | |
        C V C V C V C
```

Other examples which illustrate the same point but involve further complications appear in (9). The morpheme to which reduplication applies in these cases is not the root but the continuative prefix <u>ali</u>-. Since this prefix begins with a vowel, reduplication leads to overcopying of the preceding consonantal prefix <u>s</u>- '3rd person' (see section 3.1.4 above for discussion).

(9)

    s-ali-nowon   sal-salinowon   'he is standing'

    s-ali-tap   sal-salitap   'he is coming'

3.2.1.2 Luiseño

Another example of a phonological rule which underapplies in reduplicated forms occurs in Luiseño, a Uto-Aztecan language spoken in Southern California. The basic data is found in Munro and Benson 1973, who also presented the first analysis of the underapplication phenomenon; further discussion appears in Wilbur (1973), Aronoff (1975), Davis (1976), McCarthy (1979), and Marantz (1982).

According to Munro and Benson (1973), the segments $\underline{č}$ and $\underline{š}$ in Luiseño stand in complementary distribution, with $\underline{č}$ occurring before [+cont] segments, $\underline{š}$ elsewhere. Given their complementary distribution, we can choose either segment as underlying and derive the other one by rule. I will here follow McCarthy (1979) in assuming that $\underline{š}$ is underlying and is changed to $\underline{č}$ by the rule of continuancy dissimilation given in (10).[1] As can be seen in (11), this rule gives rise to alternations between wordfinal š and prevocalic č.

(10)
$$š \longrightarrow č \:/\: \_\_ \text{[+cont]}$$

(11)
 te:ŋališ 'medicine (sg.)' kiš 'home (acc.)'
 te:ŋaličum 'medicine (pl.)' ki:ča 'home (abs.)'

The second rule involved in the Luiseño underapplication phenomenon is a rule of syncope applying quite regularly in verbal forms. Syncope (12) deletes unstressed vowels in doubly open syllables after a short stressed vowel, illustrative examples appear in (13).

(12) <u>Syncope</u> (Munro and Benson 1973)
$$V \longrightarrow \emptyset \:/\: C \acute{V} C \_\_ C V$$

(13)
 a. čáq^{w}i 'to seize' čáq^w-la 'to wrestle'
 b. páči 'to wash' páš-ku 'to leach achornflour'
  móči 'to weave' móš-la-t 'belt'

---

[1] One peculiarity of the distribution of š and č in Luiseño should be noted: in whichever direction the allophonic change is expressed, the liquids r (alveolar flap) and l must count as noncontinuants for the rule, see Munro and Benson (1973, 17) for discussion.

The forms in (13b) show that the output of Syncope is transparent with respect to rule (10), that is, the former has to precede the latter in the order of application. The alternative ordering would derive *pačku and *močlat instead of pašku and mošlat.

Munro and Benson (1973) show that the interaction of the š-č rule (10) and Syncope (12) with a certain kind of reduplication in Luiseño presents something of a puzzle. The reduplication process in question, which derives deintensive nominals from roots, is very widespread and applies to the majority of verb roots of the language. Illustrative examples appear in (14). (The final š in the reduplicated forms is the absolutive ending; Ṣ stands for a retroflex sibilant.)

(14)
ʔáva	'to be red'	ʔavá-ʔvaš	'pink'
máha	'to stop'	mahá-mhaš	'slow'
Ṣá:wa	'to wheeze'	Ṣawá-Ṣwaš	'hoarse'
láxʷa	'to have poor eyesight'	laxʷá-lxʷaš	'type of rattlesnake'
táki	'to straighten'	takí-tkiš	'straight'
piwí:	'to be grey'	piwí-pwiš	'grey'

Restating Munro and Benson's (1973) basic analysis, we can analyse this as stem-final CVCV reduplication; the original stem gets stressed on the second syllable, and

the reduplicated portion then loses its first vowel by
the rule of syncope.

The problem is that the š-č rule (10) seems to apply
in the wrong context in the reduplicated portion, namely
before noncontinuants. This is shown by the forms in (15),
where the expected forms are in fact ungrammatical (the
second example is a reduplicatum tantum).

(15)
čoka	'limp'	čuka-čka-š	'limping'	*čuka-ška-š
čañi	--	čañi-čñi-š	'having supernatural power'	*čañi-šñi-š
čara	'tear'	čara-čra-š	'torn'	*čara-šra-š

One way of accounting for these forms in the present
theory is illustrated in the derivation given in (16) for
čukáčkaš. The basic idea is that both rules, Syncope (12)
and the š-č rule (10), apply throughout the phonology,
before and after Tier Conflation, with Syncope preceding
the š-č rule in the ordering.

(16)   a. Reduplication:

```
              C V C V
              | | | |
              š o k a  +  š
              | | | |     |
              C V C V     C
```

b. Syncope: ————

c. š-č rule:
```
              C V C V
              | | | |
              č o k a  +  š
              | | | |     |
              C V C V     C
```

d. Tier Conflation:
```
              č o k a č o k a š
              | | | | | | | | |
              C V C V C V C V C
```

e. Syncope:
```
              č o k a č   k a š
              | | | | |   | | |
              C V C V C   C V C
```

f. š-č rule: ————

g. Vowel Raising: č u k á č k a š

Before Tier Conflation, Syncope cannot apply to reduplicated forms since its context is not met (16b). As a consequence the š-č rule, which is normally bled by Syncope, can apply and affricates the root-initial melody element (16c).[2] After Tier Conflation, the context of

---

[2]This presupposes that the š-č rule (10), which introduces a feature not contrastive in morpheme representations, can apply during the cyclic phonology. We can capture this formally by assuming that the filter prohibiting the marking of continuancy on palatal obstruents in morpheme representations is no longer operative at the level where reduplication takes place, so Structure Preservation does not block the application of the š-č rule (10).

Syncope is met, and the rule applies, deleting the first vowel of the reduplicated portion of the form (16e). The deletion of this vowel places the segment y̆, derived before Tier Conflation in a prevocalic environment, next to a noncontinuant. What we are dealing with, in this analysis, is underapplication of syncope in reduplicative structures. This is a more abstract case of underapplication than the one encountered in Chumash because Luiseño Syncope has a second chance to apply after Tier Conflation. The 'temporary' underapplication of Syncope, while not itself visible in the surface form, has tangible consequences for another rule, namely the š-y̆ rule.

3.2.2 Geminate blocking

As was pointed out above, there is a second way in which rules can underapply in reduplicative structures. An integral part of the Single Melody Hypothesis is the proposal that melody elements in reduplication are doubly associated - with root skeleton and reduplicative skeleton - until Tier Conflation linearizes the skeleta. We are thus dealing with 'nonlinear' geminates, and this raises an interesting question: Does the well-known Geminate

Constraint, which was formulated for linear geminates, carry over to this new species of geminates? If it does, this would provide interesting support for the Single Melody Hypothesis over all theories of reduplication which do not possess the crucial representational property.

Various versions of the Geminate Constraint have appeared in the literature (Kenstowicz and Pyle 1973, Guerssel 1978, Steriade 1982, Hayes 1986, Steriade and Schein 1984, to appear). I will here adopt the version proposed in Steriade and Schein (1984) (which is further developed in Steriade and Schein (to appear)). The proper formulation of the constraint requires some elementary rule typology, in particular a distinction between structure-dependent rules and strictly melodic rules. A phonological rule is <u>structure-dependent</u> if it involves in its structural description some reference to the skeleton or its syllabic organization. A rule which does not involve such reference but is stated purely in terms of melodic features is a <u>strictly melodic</u> rule. The constraint is given in (17) (with minor modifications in wording from Steriade & Schein (1984)).

(17)
    A structure-dependent rule which changes the feature content of a melody element can only apply if all skeletal slots to which the melody element is linked fulfill the structural description of the rule.

Geminates freely undergo strictly melodic rules, and not all structure-dependent rules are governed by the Geminate Constraint: Rules which mention both skeleton and melody but merely alter the skeletal associations of melody elements without changing their features are not blocked by the Geminate Constraint. Crucially governed by the condition in (17), then, is the class of structure-dependent melodic feature-changing rules.

For purposes of illustration, we can turn to an example already mentioned in the introduction to this chapter in the context of the discussion of Tier Conflation. Tiberian Hebrew has a rule of postvocalic spirantization given in (18).

(18)
$$\begin{bmatrix} -son \\ -CP \end{bmatrix} \longrightarrow [+cont] \quad / \quad \underset{V\ C}{\underline{\quad\top\quad}}$$

This rule affects postvocalic stops, but consistently fails to apply to geminates. The Tiberian Hebrew form in (19) is a case in point. Note that the medial geminate b is not spirantized, but the final single b is.

(19)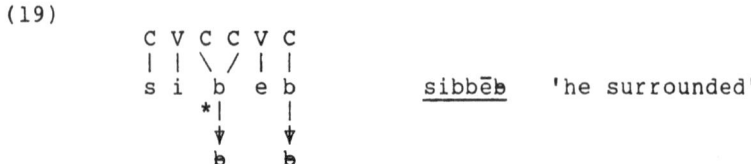

                                            sibēb   'he surrounded'

    This is a straightforward consequence of the Geminate Constraint, since only the first, but not the second, of the C-slots to which the medial b is linked fulfills the structural description of Spirantization, which requires a C immediately following a V.

    An example of rule underapplication in reduplication which can be explained as geminate blocking appears in the Austronesian language Rotuman; this case was brought to my attention by John McCarthy, and the following discussion draws heavily on his analysis.

    Rotuman morphology is characterized by a basic distinction between two 'phases', complete phase and incomplete phase, where the incomplete phase characterizes elements which are in close construction with following elements, for example possessors appear in the incomplete phase. In addition, the phase contrast is used to express distinctions in definiteness (for nouns) and tense/aspect (for verbs). Formally the incomplete phase differs from the complete phase by the absence of a final vowel and various concomitant changes affecting the remaining vowel(s). Some of the patterns are illustrated in (20) (all data are taken from Churchward 1941; some allophonic vowel modifications which do not differentiate between the two phases are not indicated in the examples).

(20)

	complete phase	incomplete phase	
a.	haga	hag	'to feed'
	hoto	hot	'to jump'
	ʔutu	ʔut	'to move'
	punu	pun	'spoon'
	leʔe	leʔ	'child'
	fisi	fis	'white'
b.	futi	fût	'to pull'
	fuʔi	fûʔ	'thunder'
	muri	mûr	'base, ramp'
	hoti	hŏt	'to embark'
	hoʔi	hŏʔ	'to return'
	pogi	pŏg	'night'
	mose	mŏs	'to sleep'
	tore	tŏr	'to remain'
c.	pure	pu͡er	'to decide'
	hosa	ho͡as	'flower'
	piko	pi͡ok	'lazy'
	lima	li͡am	'five'
	pepa	pe͡ap	'paper'
	luka	lu͡ak	'short'
d.	hagu	hag	'to awaken'
	kopu	kop	'to flood'
	seru	ser	'comb'
	faʔo	faʔ	'nail'
	heʔo	heʔ	'to call'
	folu	fol	'three'

The principles responsible for the changes in vocalism observable in the incomplete phase forms are quite clearly stated in Churchward (1941, 80). When the complete phase has two identical vowels (20a), the second vowel disappears in the incomplete phase (e.g. haga/hag). When the complete phase has two different vowels, the form of the incomplete phase depends on the nature of the vowels. If the vowels are u + i, o + i, or o + e (20b), the incomplete phase shows an umlauted version of the first vowel (e.g. futi/füt). Otherwise, the final vowel apparently metathesizes with the preceding consonant to form a short diphthong with the precedent vowel (indicated by a ligature in (20c)), as in pure/pu͡er, provided the final vowel is lower than the preceding vowel. Otherwise, the final vowel is dropped (20d). This description does not exhaust the vowel changes in the incomplete phase but is sufficient for our present purposes.

Following Saito's (1981) and McCarthy's (1986) analyses in most respects, we can understand these phenomena in the following way. The fundamental assumption is that vowels and consonants occupy different tiers in Rotuman. The examples in (20a) then have a single vowel melody, and nothing happens in the incomplete phase: Since there is only a single vowel slot available in the incomplete phase, the vowel is singly associated, as illustrated in (21).

(21)
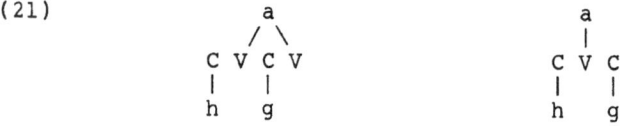

Short diphthongs are derived by a reassociation rule (22) associating the core of a floating vocalic melody element to a preceding vowel slot, provided the floating vowel (indicated by the circled core) is lower in height than the preceding vowel.

(22)   Short Diphthong Formation

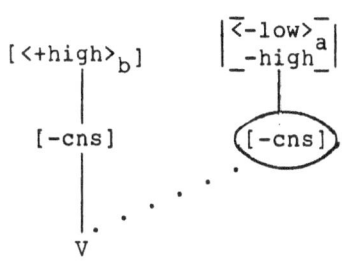

If a then b

Departing from McCarthy's (1986) analysis, Umlaut is stated in (23) as a rule linking the [-back] feature of a vowel melody which is not attached to the skeleton to the core of a preceding nonlow back vowel, simultaneously delinking the feature [+back].

(23)   Umlaut

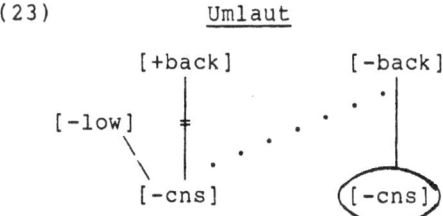

In McCarthy's (1986, 215) description of the Umlaut process umlauted vowels go through a diphthongal stage in which the umlaut-triggers i and e share a V-slot with the preceding vowel. The Umlaut rule itself is then stated as a coalescence operation affecting certain pairs of vowel melodies associated with the same V position. For example, the incomplete phase form mös is derived as indicated in (24).

(24)
```
      o e              o e              ö
      |                |/               |
    C V C     -->    C V C     -->    C V C
    |   |            |   |            |   |
    m   s            m   s            m   s
```

This way of deriving umlauted vowels runs into problems in cases where Umlaut applies to multiply-linked vowel melodies (e.g. pulufi 'stick', incompl. phase pülüf), as shown in (25): If Umlaut is stated as a coalescence rule applying to short diphthongs, the application of the rule in (25) violates the Geminate Constraint because the vowel melody u is not exclusively anchored in the V-slot that it shares with the umlaut trigger i.

(25)
```
        u   i            u   i             ü
       / \              / \ /             / \
     C V C V C   -->  C V C V C   -->   C V C V C
     |   |   |        |   |   |         |   |   |
     p   l   f        p   l   f         p   l   f
```

Our formulation in (23) avoids this problem, since it does not stipulate anything about the skeletal affiliations of the umlaut-undergoing vowel and lets the rule be triggered by floating i and e.

If Short Diphthong Formation (22) precedes Umlaut (23) in the ordering of rules, we do not have to impose a restriction on the Umlaut rule to prevent e from umlauting a preceding u, since (22) will always bleed away this potential application of (23).

It is clear that the Umlaut rule must make reference to the skeleton and cannot be stated as a purely melodic process, since it is only triggered by e and i not associated with a V slot of their own. Note also that Umlaut (23) changes the feature content of melody elements, unlike Short Diphthong Formation (22), which performs a reassociation operation between melody and skeleton while leaving the melody elements themselves unaltered. These points will be of crucial importance below.

Short Diphthong Formation (22) and Umlaut (23) account for the vocalism of the incomplete phase forms in (20b,c) above. This is shown in (26) for one representative example from each group.

(26)

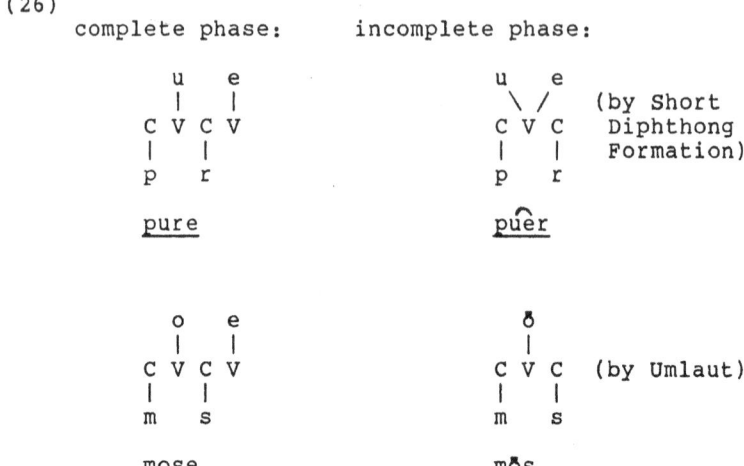

Compounds in Rotuman are governed by strict laws regulating the phases of their members. Non-heads (first elements) always take the incomplete phase, whereas heads (second elements) appear in the complete or the incomplete phase, depending on the syntactic environment of the whole compound.

Reduplication serves a variety of morphological functions in Rotuman, it expresses frequentative, continuative, and pejorative meanings and is in addition used to derive adjectives from nouns and verbs. Reduplication is partial and reduplicates the initial CVC sequence, as is clear from the reduplicated forms of trisyllabic (and longer) words in (27).

(27)

sakiro	sak-sakiro	'to scrutinize'
hununuka	hun-hununuka	'to gasp for breath'
fe?eni	fe?-fe?eni	'zealous'
unoku	un-unoku	'to protrude'

Reduplicated forms are governed by the phase laws holding for all compounds. Consider (28), which shows reduplicated forms in their two possible shapes, with the second (head) element in the complete phase (left-hand column) and with the second element in the incomplete phase (right-hand column). The first element is in the incomplete phase in all cases.

(28)

	head in complete phase	head in incomplete phase	
a.	hag-haga	hag-hag	'to feed'
	mat-mata	mat-mat	'wet'
	?ut-?utu	?ut-?ut	'to move'
	sek-seke	sek-sek	'to stroll'
b.	mos-mose	mŏs-mŏs	'to sleep'
	hot-hoti	hŏt-hŏt	'to embark'
	ho?-ho?i	hŏ?-hŏ?	'to return'
	fut-futi	fŭt-fŭt	'to pull'

c. tôak-toka   tôak-tôak 'to cease'
   púer-pure   púer-púer 'to decide'
   méa?-me?a   méa?-méa? 'small'
   jíak-jika   jíak-jíak 'narrow'

The forms on the right, where both compound members are in the incomplete phase, are unremarkable, the phase phonology shows all its usual effects (with umlauted vowels and short diphthongs). But among the forms on the left, where the phases of the compound members differ, there is one surprising group of forms, namely those in (28b). The expected incomplete phase forms of the first members are mös, höt, hö?, and füt, with Umlaut (see (20b)). This underapplication of Umlaut is a systematic characteristic of reduplicated forms whose parts stand in different phases. On the other hand, Short Diphthong Formation does not underapply in reduplicated forms with phase differences, as evidenced by the forms in (28c).

The proper way of understanding the underapplication of Umlaut involves an appeal to the Geminate Constraint. Consider the representations in (29a-f). For perspicuity I have indicated only the vowel melodies and their associations.

(29)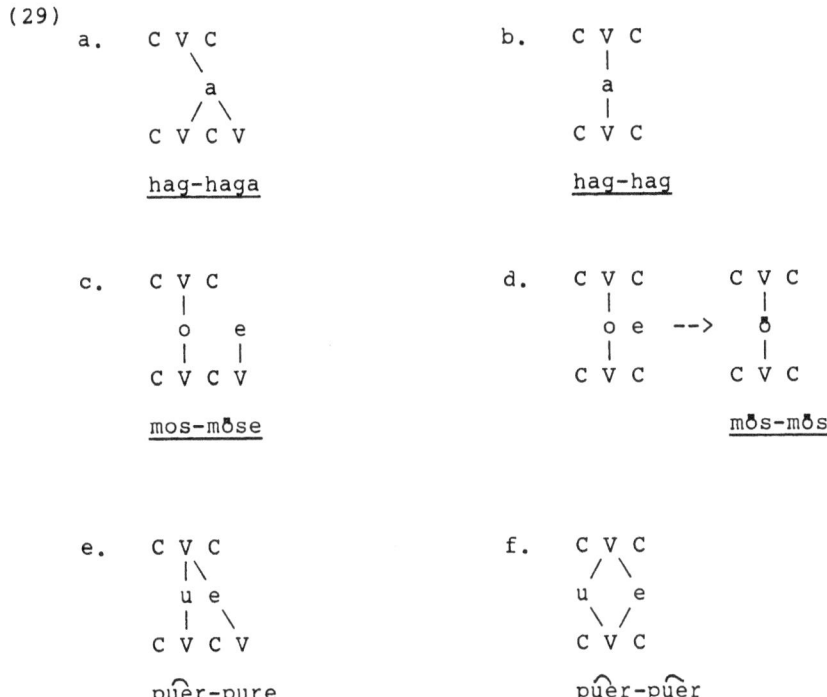

The representation (29c) makes clear how the Geminate Constraint blocks the application of Umlaut and thus accounts for the underapplication effect. The vowel e is floating with respect to the reduplicative skeleton - this part of the representation fulfills the structural description of Umlaut (23). But the same melody element e is also associated to a V slot in the root skeleton. This is a configuration to which the Geminate Constraint is sensitive, and the rule blocks. When the melody element e is floating with respect to both skeleta, as in (29d), the application of Umlaut (23) does not violate the Geminate Constraint and the rule applies, deriving <u>mös-mös</u>.

Different from Umlaut (23), Short Diphthong Formation (22) does not change melody features but merely adds an association line between melody and skeketon. The Geminate Constraint is irrelevant for pure association rules of this kind, and we therefore predict that Short Diphthong Formation (22) should take place freely in reduplicative compounds whose members differ in phase. This prediction is borne out by the forms in (28c). Association can thus take place differently between the melody and the two skeleta, as in (29e) <u>puêr-pure</u>, but a feature change in the shared melody like Umlaut can only take place uniformly, i.e. when both parts are in the incomplete phase, as in (29d) mös-mös, otherwise it is blocked by the Geminate Constraint, as in (29c) <u>mos-mose</u>.

Geminate blocking effects of this kind in reduplicative constructions crucially presuppose the existence of a shared melody. Notice that other nonconcatenative approaches to reduplication do not posit doubly linked single melodies. In Clements' (1985) model the reduplicative skeleton is associated with the <u>skeleton</u> of the base, as schematically indicated in (30), with subsequent <u>transfer</u> of the melody and linearization.

(30)

At no point in this derivation is a single melody element associated with two synchronous skeleton elements: Before melody transfer, ta is only associated with the base skeleton; after melody transfer, we have two copies of ta. Consequently no appeal to the Geminate Constraint is possible in this model.[3]

If reduplication is viewed as involving a strict across-the-board (ATB) representation, with both skeleton and melody represented in parallel (Uhrbach 1985; see Hirschbühler 1978 for an earlier ATB-proposal in an SPE-style framework), a reduplicated form would be represented as in (31):

___

[3] The primary objective of the model of reduplication proposed in Clements (1985) is not the explanation of over/underapplication of rules in reduplication, but rather the explanation of transfer effects, i.e. cases where the association relations between melody and root skeleton are preserved in reduplicative association and for example long vowels are copied as long. For the theory developed in this chapter, I assume that such phenomena are to be accounted for by imposing symmetry constraints on the association relations between the melody and the two skeleta.

(31)
$$\begin{vmatrix} \overline{C} & \overline{V} \\ | & | \\ t & a \\ & & C & V \\ C & V & | & | \\ | & | & p & a \\ \underline{t} & \underline{a} \end{vmatrix}$$

Before linearization, we have parallelism between the parts of the reduplicated form, but no connection, and in particular no double association of melody elements. So again the Geminate Constraint can have no influence on the phonological behavior of reduplicated forms.

In order to account for the fact that in Rotuman the (feature-changing) Umlaut rule underapplies in reduplicated forms, but not the (purely associative) rule of Short Diphthong Formation, both the transfer model and the ATB model would have to stipulate a separate condition. For theory of reduplication proposed in this chapter, the difference follows from a difference in rule type and the fact that the representation contains a single melody associated with two skeleta.

3.3 Further Single-Melody Effects: Sanskrit Deaspiration

In this section I would like to show that there are further single melody effects which support the hypothesis that reduplication involves the existence of a single melody shared by two synchronous skeleta. In certain cases, processes which are restricted to occur only inside morphemes seem to apply across a morpheme boundary just in reduplicated forms and nowhere else. That is, the total melody of reduplicative morpheme plus root acts as if it constitutes a single morpheme. Grassmann's Law in Sanskrit is a well-known case of this kind. A root with two underlying aspirates like /$b^h u d^h$/ 'to understand' in (1) loses the aspiration on its first consonant by Grassmann's Law, as shown by the present tense form $bod^h ati$ in (1a).

(1)
    a.   /$b^h u d^h$/   'understand'
         bod^h-ati (present)
         $b^h ot$-syati (future)

    b.   /$b^h id$/   'split'
         $b^h i$-$b^h id$ --> bi-$b^h id$ (perfect)

If, however, the second root consonant is deaspirated by an independent process, as in the future form $b^h otsyati$,

Grassmann's Law does not apply, and the first root consonant remains aspirated. The reduplicated perfect of /b^hid/ 'to split, to break' in (1b) shows that Grassmann's Law applies to reduplicated consonants, which are always deaspirated.

The significant point is that Grassmann's Law never applies across any other morpheme boundary, as from suffix to root, or between compound members. In particular, aspirates in prefixes do not lose their aspiration by Grassmann's Law, as shown by the forms in (2).

(2)
    $ab^h i$-$g^h r\bar{a}$ 'smell'
    $ab^h i$-$d^h a$ 'tell, speak'
    $ab^h i$-$b^h \bar{u}$ 'overpower'

We are thus dealing with a root-internal process which extends into reduplication. Grassmann's Law is not an isolated phenomenon with these characteristics, Deglottalization in Shuswap and other Salish languages has virtually identical characteristics (see Gibson 1973, Kuipers 1974, and in particular Thompson and Thompson 1985).

We are now faced with two questions. First, how do we express the notion "root-internal", given the fact that Grassmann's Law applies not on the root cycle, but much

later in the derivation, as evidenced by the form
b^hotsyati? Second, is there a principled explanation for
the fact that Grassmann's Law applies to reduplicated
forms? A number of previous analyses (e.g. the one
presented in Borowsky and Mester 1983) did not give a
unified account for the loss of aspiration in the root
and in reduplication, and this is quite unsatisfactory,
since it appears that a significant generalization has
been missed.

The first question can be answered if we assume a
prosodic analysis of Sanskrit aspiration, following a long
tradition of research (Harris 1944, Allen 1951, Steriade
1982, Borowsky and Mester 1983, Kaye and Lowenstamm 1985).
The roots /b^hud^h/ and /b^hid/ will then be represented as
in (3a) and (3b), where H is the aspiration autosegment.

(3)

The Obligatory Contour Principle (OCP) forces the
structure in (3a) with a branching aspiration autosegment
for diaspirate roots. We then get a representational
difference between successive aspirates within a root and
successive aspirates across morpheme boundary: only the
former will be represented by multiple association, as

in (3a). In other words, being linked to one and the same aspiration element is a prosodic characteristic of consonants which are part of the same root. We can now formulate Grassmann's Law so as to refer to this prosodic characteristic. This is a welcome result since we can avoid reference to the morphological category "root" at later stages of the derivation. In (4) the rule is stated as an operation delinking a doubly linked aspiration autosegment from its first anchor. I asssume that the aspiration autosegment is associated to the core of the melody and that Grassmann's Law (4) applies at the word level. Since the delinking rule in (4) refers to multiply associated aspiration, the rule will not apply across morpheme boundaries, as desired, and we do not have to impose a special restriction.

(4)   Grassmann's Law (GL)

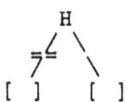

The derivations of bod^hati and ab^hi-d^ha are sketched below. In (5a) Grassmann's Law applies to the doubly associated aspiration in the root and deaspirates the first root consonant b. In (5b), however, the structural description of Grassmann's Law is not met - there is no doubly associated aspiration -, and both b and d remain aspirated.

(5)
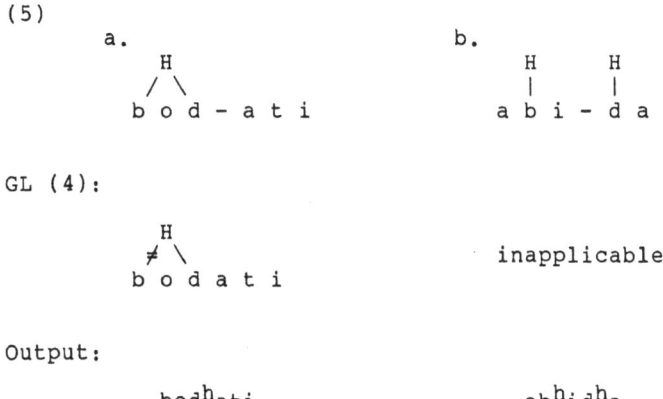

GL (4):

```
     H
    ≠ \
    b o d a t i
```
inapplicable

Output:

bod^{h}ati   ab^{h}id^{h}a

Consider also the case where the second root consonant is devoiced and deaspirated by an independently necessary local assimilation process.

(6)
```
              H
             / \
           b o d - s y a t i
```

local assimilation
of laryngeal features:
```
              H
             /
           b o t s y a t i
```

Grassmann's Law: inapplicable
(4)

Output: b^{h}otsyati

In (6), the second root consonant assimilates to the suffix-initial s in laryngeal features and appears as t. Since there is no longer a doubly associated aspiration, Grassmann's Law does not apply, and the first root consonant remains aspirated.

Given this analysis of Grassmann's Law, we can now address our second question: Why does Grassmann's Law apply in reduplication, but in no other heteromorphemic context? It turns out that this question finds a principled answer in the approach to reduplication outlined in this chapter, which posits a single melody associated to two synchronous skeleta and makes use of the independently motivated principle of Tier Conflation to linearize the skeleta.

The interesting case is the reduplicated perfect of b^hid 'to split', whose derivation is given in (7) below: The melodic core of the first root consonant is doubly associated in the reduplicated form, with the aspiration autosegment linked to the melodic core. Tier Conflation applies to this representation and rewrites the first consonant-vowel sequence, to avoid crossing of association lines. But Tier Conflation crucially does not rewrite the aspiration autosegment (there is no reason to do so), and we get a linearized representation with a doubly associated aspiration autosegment. This representation meets the structural description of Grassmann's Law (4), which applies after Tier Conflation and delinks the aspiration from the first consonant.

(7)
$$\begin{array}{c} H \\ \backslash \\ b\ i\ d \\ |\ \ |\ \ | \\ C\ V\ C \end{array}$$

Reduplication:
$$\begin{array}{c} H \\ \ \ \backslash\quad C\ V \\ \ \ \backslash /\ / \\ b\ i\ d \\ |\ \ |\ \ | \\ C\ V\ C \end{array}$$

Tier Conflation:
$$\begin{array}{c} H \\ /\ \backslash \\ b\ i\ b\ i\ d \\ |\ \ |\ \ |\ \ |\ \ | \\ C\ V\ C\ V\ C \end{array}$$

Grassmann's Law:
(4)
$$\begin{array}{c} H \\ \not\ \backslash \\ b\ i\ b\ i\ d \\ |\ \ |\ \ |\ \ |\ \ | \\ C\ V\ C\ V\ C \end{array}$$

Output: $\underline{bib^hid}$

3.4 Post-Conflation Rules

In the theory presented here, rule overapplication and rule underapplication are both consequences of the fact that reduplicative structures involve melody elements which are doubly associated. This type of representation is preserved until Tier Conflation linearizes the structure. This makes a clear prediction for rules which follow Tier Conflation, in particular for all postlexical rules: They should never have overapplication or underapplication effects; rather, they should always apply in the normal way wherever their linear context is met, and reduplicated forms should not be special in any way, as far as postlexical rules are concerned. This prediction seems to be borne out by the evidence; in the preceding sections we already encountered some postlexical processes which applied to reduplicated forms without over- or underapplying. One interesting example is the Sanskrit ruki rule, which applies both before and after Tier Conflation. As pointed out in section 3.1.2 above, overapplication effects are exclusively found in preconflational applications of ruki.

To further illustrate this point, I will return to Dakota (Shaw 1976). Dakota has a rule of Cluster Simplification (1) formulated as a skeletal rule which deletes the first element of a triconsonantal cluster.

(1) Cluster Simplification

　　　C ---> ∅ / __ CC

As shown by the reduplicated forms in (2) (this is final syllable reduplication, and the a is added by an epenthesis rule), Cluster Simplification applies to the first part of a reduplicative construction and deletes a consonant before two consonants (for example, the first p in ksap-ksap-a). The corresponding consonant in the second part is not affected by this deletion, nor does it block the deletion in the first part.

(2)
　　ksap-ksap-a　　--->　　ksa-ksap-a　　'be wise'
　　blez-blez-a　　--->　　ble-blez-a　　'be sane'

A second postlexical rule which applies in this way is a general rule deaspirating and deglottalizing consonants in preconsonantal position. The rule is given in (3), and (4) illustrates its operation. Note again that the final k? of the root melody ends up deglottalized in the first part, but glottalized in the second part of the reduplicated form.

(3) Preconsonantal Deglottalization/Deaspiration

   [laryngeal features]
          |
         =╪=
          |
   [+cons]   [+cons]

(4) 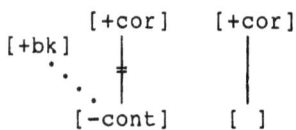 'little, small'

Shaw (1976) points out that Dakota Palatalization, which in our terms precedes Tier Conflation and overapplies in reduplicated forms (section 3.1.1), interacts in a rather interesting way with two rules which follow Tier Conflation. The first of these, (5), is a rule dissimilating the coronals t č l n to k if they precede another coronal.

(5) Coronal Dissimilation

            [+cor]   [+cor]
    [+bk] | |
      ·.   ╪ |
       ·. | |
          [-cont]   [ ]

The second rule, (6), lenites the coronal obstruents č and t to l in the syllable coda.

(6) Coronal Lenition

$$\begin{bmatrix} +\text{cor} \\ \begin{bmatrix} -\text{son} \\ -\text{cont} \end{bmatrix} \\ \text{C} \end{bmatrix}_\sigma \longrightarrow [+\text{son}]$$

A root like kʰeč̌ 'to be similar to' in (7) with an initial velar and a final palatal appears in drastically different shapes when reduplicated, depending on whether or not Palatalization has applied.

(7) /kʰeč̌/   'to be similar to'

   he-č̌ʰek-č̌ʰeč̌-a   'it is like that'

   ka-kʰel-kʰeč̌-a   'it is like that yonder'

Thus we get he-č̌ʰek-č̌ʰeč̌-a 'it is like that' with the front-vowel prefix he, which triggers Palatalization, but ka-kʰel-kʰeč̌-a 'it is like that yonder' with the back vowel prefix ka. These forms are derived as in (8).

(8)

a. Reduplication,
Prefixation:

```
                      C V C                           C V C
                      | | |                           | | |
          h             h                               h
      h e + k  e č + a                     k a + k  e č + a
      | |   | | | |                        | |   | | | |
      C V   C V C V                        C V   C V C V
```

b. Velar
Palatalization:

```
                      C V C
                      | | |
                       h
          h e + čh e č + a                  -------
          | |   | | | |
          C V   C V C V
```

c. Tier
Conflation:

```
              h e čh e č čh e č a           k a kh e č kh e č a
              | | | | | | | | |             | | | | | | | | |
              C V C V C C V C V             C V C V C C V C V
```

d. Coronal
Dissimilation: h e čh e k čh e č a   ---------

e. Coronal
Lenition: -------   k a kh e l kh e č a

3.5 Conclusion

In this chapter, we have pursued the Single Melody Theory of reduplication, which is built on three central hypotheses:

(i) Reduplicative templates are morphemes synchronous with the base skeleton.

(ii) Reduplicative templates are directly associated with the base melody, and reduplicated forms are thus characterized by a single melody associated with two skeleta.

(iii) The linearization of such representations is an instance of Tier Conflation, which takes place at the end of each lexical level.

This model offers a natural explanation for the unexpected application and nonapplication of phonological rules in reduplicated structures. Since Tier Conflation is confined to the end of lexical levels, phonological rules which apply to reduplicated forms at their level of formation receive as their inputs representations with melody elements associated with two simultaneous skeleta. It was argued that such rules have overapplication effects if they strictly affect the shared melody (melodic overapplication) or in addition the prosodic organization of the two simultaneous skeleta (skeletal overapplication). Underapplication effects are found in two sets of circumstances. First, when one part of the reduplicated form would have to provide the context necessary for the rule to apply to the other part. The context of the rule is then simply not met inside the reduplicative construction, whose parts are not linearized before Tier Conflation. The second kind underapplication is an instantiation of geminate blocking. Before Tier Conflation shared melody elements in reduplicated forms are part of nonlinear geminate structures, and rule application to such structures is governed by the Geminate Constraint. A necessary condition for over- and underapplication effects is access to the nonconflated representation of reduplicated forms, so we predict that rules applying after Tier Conflation, in particular postlexical rules, cannot overapply or underapply. The strength of this theory of reduplication is that it can account for some of the unexpected phonological behavior of reduplicative constructions in a minimally stipulative way, utilizing independently motivated principles of nonlinear phonological theory such as Tier Conflation and the condition on multiply-linked structures.

BIBLIOGRAPHY

Allen, W. S. (1951) "Some Prosodic Aspects of Retroflexion and Aspiration in Sanskrit," BSOAS 13, 936-46.

Anderson, J. M. and C. Jones (1974) "Three Theses concerning Phonological Representations," Journal of Linguistics 10, 1-26.

Anderson, J. M. and C. Jones (1977) Phonological Structure and the History of English, North-Holland Publishing Company, Amsterdam.

Applegate, R. (1976) "Reduplication in Chumash," in Langour and Silver, eds., 271-83.

Archangeli, D. (1984) Underspecification in Yawelmani Phonology and Morphology, Doctoral dissertation, MIT, Cambridge, Mass.

Archangeli, D. (1985) "Yokuts Harmony: Evidence for Coplanar Representation in Nonlinear Phonology," Linguistic Inquiry 16, 335-72.

Aronoff, M. (1975) Word Formation in Generative Grammar, MIT Press, Cambridge, Massachusetts, and London, England.

Bloomfield, L. (1933) Language, Holt, New York.

Borowsky, T. and R. A. Mester (1983) "Aspiration to Roots," Proceedings of CLS 19, 52-63.

Broselow, E. and J. J. McCarthy (1984) "A Theory of Internal Reduplication," The Linguistic Review 3, 25-88.

Carrier, J. L. (1979) The Interaction of Morphological and Phonological Rules in Tagalog, Doctoral dissertation, MIT, Cambridge, Massachusetts.

Chiri, M. (1952) "Ainugo ni okeru boin chowa (Vowel Harmony in the Ainu Language)," Hokkaido University Bulletin in Humanities 1, 101-18. Reprinted in Chiri Mashio Zenshuu [Collected Works of Mashio Chiri], Vol. 4, 201-225, Heibonsha, Tokyo (1984).

Chomsky, N. and M. Halle (1968) *The Sound Pattern of English*, Harper and Row, New York.

Churchward, C. M. (1941) *Rotuman Grammar and Dictionary*, Australasia Medical Publishing Company, Sydney.

Churma, D. (1984) "On Explaining Morpheme Structure," *Ohio State University Working Papers in Linguistics* 29, 12-29.

Clements, G. N. (1976) *Vowel Harmony in Nonlinear Generative Phonology*. Published in 1980 by Indiana University Linguistics Club.

Clements, G.N. (1977) "Neutral Vowels in Hungarian Vowel Harmony, An Autosegmental Interpretation," in J.A. Kegl, D. Nash, and A. Zaenen, eds., *Proceedings of the Seventh Annual Meeting of the North Eastern Linguistic Society*, MIT, Cambridge, Massachusetts.

Clements, G.N. (1981) "Akan Vowel Harmony: A Nonlinear Analysis," in G.N. Clements, ed., *Harvard Studies in Phonology II*, Indiana University Linguistics Club, Bloomington, Indiana.

Clements, G. N. (1982) "A Remark on the Elsewhere Condition," *Linguistic Inquiry* 13, 682-5.

Clements, G. N. (1985) "The Problem of Transfer in Nonlinear Phonology," *Cornell Working Papers in Linguistics* 7, Cornell University, Ithaca, New York, 1-36.

Clements, G. N. (1985) "The Geometry of Phonological Features," in *Phonology Yearbook* 2, 225-52.

Clements, G. N. and S. J. Keyser (1983) *CV Phonology: A Generative Theory of the Syllable*, MIT Press, Cambridge, Massachusetts.

Clements, G.N. and E. Sezer (1982) "Vowel and Consonant Disharmony in Turkish," in H. van der Hulst and N. Smith, eds., *The structure of phonological representations*, Part II, Foris, Dordrecht and Cinnaminson, 213-55.

Cowper, E. and K. Rice (1985) "Phonology and Reduplication," ms., University of Toronto, Canada. [Paper presented at the Canadian Linguistics Association, June 1985.]

Davis, J. F. (1976) "Some Notes on Luiseño Phonology," *IJAL* 42, 192-216.

Dempwolff, O. (1934-1938) *Vergleichende Lautlehre des austronesischen Wortschatzes*. 1. Induktiver Aufbau einer indonesischen Ursprache, *Zeitschrift für Eingeborenensprachen* (ZES), Beiheft 15 (1934); 2. Deduktive Anwendung des Urindonesischen auf austronesische Einzelsprachen, ZES 17 (1937); 3. Austronesisches Wörterverzeichnis, ZES 19 (1938). Berlin.

Dudas, K. (1976) *The Phonology and Morphology of Modern Javanese*. Doctoral dissertation, University of Illinois, Urbana, Illinois.

Ewen, C. J. (1982) "The Phonological Representation of the Welsh Mutations," in J. Anderson, ed., *Language Form and Linguistic Variation*, Benjamins B.V., Amsterdam, 75-95.

Georgopoulos, C. (1982) "An Autosegmental Model for Reduplication," ms., University of California, San Diego.

Gibson, J. H. (1973) *Shuswap Grammatical Structure*. University of Hawaii Working Papers 5.5.

Goldsmith, J. (1976) *Autosegmental Phonology*, Doctoral dissertation, MIT, Cambridge, Massachusetts. [Distributed by the Indiana University Linguistics Club, Bloomington.]

Goldsmith, J. (1979) "The Aims of Autosegmental Theory," in D. A. Dinnsen, ed., *Current Approaches to Phonological Theory*, Indiana University Press, Bloomington and London.

Goldsmith, J. (1981) "Subsegmentals in Spanish Phonology: An Autosegmental Approach," in W. W. Cressey and D. J. Napoli, eds., *Linguistic Studies in the Romance Languages* 9, Georgetown University Press, Washington, D.C.

Greenberg, J. (1960) "The patterning of root morphemes in Semitic," *Word* 6, 162-81.

Guerssel, M. (1978) "A Condition on Assimilation Rules," *Linguistic Analysis* 20, 225-54.

Halle, M. and J.-R. Vergnaud (1980) "Three Dimensional Phonology," *Linguistic Research* 1, 83-105.

Harris, Z. S. (1944) "Simultaneous Components in Phonology," *Language* 20, 181-205.

Hayes, B. (1986) "Inalterability in CV Phonology," *Language* 62, 321-51.

Hayes, B. (1986a) "Assimilation as Spreading in Toba Batak," *Linguistic Inquiry* 17, 467-99.

Hirschbühler, P. (1978) "Reduplication in Javanese," *U.Mass Occasional Papers in Linguistics* 3, 102-25.

Horne, E. C. (1961) *Introductory Javanese*. Yale University Press, New Haven and London.

Itô, J. (1984) "Melodic dissimilation in Ainu," *Linguisitic Inquiry* 15, 505-13.

Itô, J. (1986) *Syllable Theory in Prosodic Phonology*, Doctoral dissertation, University of Mass. at Amherst, Amherst, Massachusetts.

Itô, J. and R.-A. Mester (1986) "The Phonology of Voicing in Japanese," Linguistic Inquiry 17, 49-73.

Johnson, C. D. (1980) "Regular Disharmony in Kirghiz," in R. Vago, ed., *Issues in Vowel Harmony*, Benjamins B.V., Amsterdam, 89-99.

Kaye, J. and J. Lowenstamm (1985) "A Non-Linear Treatment of Grassmann's Law," *Proceedings of NELS* 15, pp. 220-33.

Kenstowicz, M. (1979) "Chukchee Vowel Harmony and Epenthesis," in *The Elements*, Chicago Linguistics Society, University of Chicago, Chicago, Illinois, 402-13.

Kenstowicz, M. (1986) "Multiple Linking in Javanese," *Proceedings of NELS* 16, 230-48.

Kenstowicz, M. and C. Kisseberth (1979) *Generative Phonology*, Academic Press, New York.

Kenstowicz, M. and C. Pyle (1973) "On the Phonological Integrity of Geminate Clusters," in M. Kenstowicz and C. Kisseberth, eds., <u>Issues in Phonological Theory</u>, Mouton, The Hague.

Kiparsky, P. (1982) "Lexical Phonology and Morphology," in I.-S. Yang, ed., <u>Linguistics in the Morning Calm</u>, Linguistic Society of Korea, Hanshin, Seoul, 3-91.

Kitagawa, Y. (1984) "Three-dimensional Approach to Reduplication," unpublished paper, U.Mass., Amherst, Massachusetts.

Kitagawa, Y. (to appear) "Redoing Reduplication: A Preliminary Sketch," in G. Huck and A. Ojeda, eds., <u>Syntax and Semantics</u> vol. 20, Academic Press, New York.

Kuipers, A. H. (1974) <u>The Shuswap Language: Grammar, Texts, Dictionary</u>. Janua Linguarum Series Practica 225, Mouton, The Hague.

Kuroda, S.-Y. (1967) <u>Yawelmani Phonology</u>, MIT Press, Cambridge, Massachusetts.

Leben, W. (1973) <u>Suprasegmental Phonology</u>, Doctoral dissertation, MIT, Cambridge, Massachusetts. [Published 1979 by Garland Press, New York.]

Levin, J. (1983) "Reduplication and Prosodic Structure," ms., MIT, Cambridge, Massachusetts.

Levin, J. (1985) <u>A Metrical Theory of Syllabicity</u>, Doctoral dissertation, MIT, Cambridge, Massachusetts.

Marantz, A. (1982) "Re Reduplication," <u>Linguistic Inquiry</u> 13, 435-82.

McCarthy, J. J. (1979) <u>Formal Problems in Semitic Phonology and Morphology</u>, Doctoral dissertation, MIT, Cambridge, Massachusetts.

McCarthy, J. J. (1981) "A Prosodic Theory of Nonconcatenative Morphology," <u>Linguistic Inquiry</u> 12, 373-413.

McCarthy, J. J. (1983) "Consonant Morphology in the Chaha Verb," in M. Barlow, D. Flickinger, and M. Wescoat, eds., *Proceedings of the West Coast Conference on Formal Linguistics*, Stanford Linguistics Association, Stanford, California.

McCarthy, J. J. (1985) "Features and Tiers: Semitic Root Structure Constraints Revisited," talk delivered at the University of Illinois at Urbana, Oct. 1985.

McCarthy, J. J. (1986) "OCP Effects: Gemination and Antigemination," *Linguistic Inquiry* 17, 207-63.

McCarthy, J. J. (ms.) "Some notes on ATB Phonology," AT&T Bell Labatories, Murray Hill, New Jersey.

McCarthy, J. J. and A. Prince (1985) "Dissecting the Skeleton," paper delivered at the 1985 West Coast Conference on Formal Linguistics.

McCarthy, J. J. and A. Prince (in preparation) "Prosodic Morphology."

Mohanan, K. P. (1981) *Lexical Phonology*, Doctoral dissertation, MIT, Cambridge, Massachusetts.

Mohanan, K. P. (1983) "The Structure of the Melody," ms., MIT and National University of Singapore.

Munro, P. and P. Benson (1973) "Reduplication and Rule Ordering in Luiseño," *IJAL* 39, 15-21.

Newman, S. (1944) *Yokuts Language of California*, Viking Fund Publications in Anthropology No. 2, New York.

Nothofer, B. (1975) *The Reconstruction of Proto-Malayo-Javanic*, M. Nijnhoff, 'S-Gravenhage.

Pesetsky, D. (1979) "Russian Morphology and Lexical Theory," ms., MIT, Cambridge, Massachusetts.

Plenat, M. (1982) "Toto, Guiguite, Totor, Fanfa et toute la famille," paper presented at GLOW colloquium, Paris.

Prince, A. (1983) "Relating to the Grid," *Linguistic Inquiry* 14, 19-100.

Prince, A. (1984) "Phonology with Tiers," in M. Aronoff and R. Oehrle, eds., <u>Language Sound Structure</u>, MIT Press, Cambridge, Massachusetts, 234-244.

Prince, A. (to appear) "Planes and Copying," <u>Linguistic Inquiry</u>.

Rehg, K. L. and D. G. Sohl (1981) <u>Ponapean Reference Grammar</u>, The University Press of Hawaii, Honolulu, Hawaii.

Saito, M. (1981) "A Preliminary Account of the Rotuman Vowel System," ms., MIT, Cambridge, Massachusetts.

Sapir, E. (1930) <u>Southern Paiute, a Shoshonean Language</u>. Proceedings of the American Academy of Arts and Sciences 65, nos. 1-3.

Schlindwein, D. (1986) "Tier Alignment in Reduplication," <u>Proceedings of NELS</u> 16, 419-33.

Steriade, D. (ms.) "Parameters of Metrical Vowel Harmony Rules," MIT, Cambridge, Mass.

Steriade, D. (1982) <u>Greek Prosodies and the Nature of Syllabification</u>, Doctoral dissertation, MIT, Cambridge, Massachusetts.

Steriade, D. and B. Schein (1984) "Geminates and Structure-Dependent Rules," in <u>Proceedings of the Third West Coast Conference on Formal Linguistics</u>, 263-91.

Steriade, D. and B. Schein (to appear) "On Geminates," <u>Linguistic Inquiry</u>.

Stevens, A. M. (1968) <u>Madurese Phonology and Morphology</u>, American Oriental Society Series Vol. 52, American Oriental Society, New Haven, Connecticut.

Stevens, A.M. (1985) "Reduplication in Madurese," in <u>Cuny Forum</u> #11, 92-102.

Thomas, J. M. C. (1963) <u>Le parler ngbaka de Bokanga: Phonologie, morphologie, syntax</u>. Mouton and Co, Paris and La Haye.

Thomas, J. M. C. (1970) <u>Contes Ngbaka - Ma'bo</u>. Editions Klincksieck, Paris.

Thompson, L. C. and M. T. Thompson (1985) "A Grassmann's Law for Salish," in *Festschrift for Gordon Fairbanks*, 134-47.

Tucker, A.N. (1969) Review of Burssens, A. (1969) *Problemen en inventarisatie van de verbale strukturen in het dho alur (Noordoost-Kongo)*, Brussels, *Journal of African Languages* 8, 125-6.

Tuller, L (1981) "On Nominal Inflection in Hausa," in Thomas-Flinders, T. ed., *UCLA Occasional Papers #4: Working Papers in Morphology*, 117-157.

Uhlenbeck, E. M. (1949) *De Structuur van het Javaanse Morpheem*, Nix & Co, Bandoeng.

Uhlenbeck, E. M. (1950) "The Structure of the Javanese Morpheme," *Lingua* 2, 239-70. [Reprinted in E. C. Hamp, F. W. Householder, and R. Austerlitz, eds., *Readings in Linguistics* II, The University of Chicago Press, Chicago and London, 248-70.]

Uhrbach, A. (1984) "Some Comments on Reduplication and Morphology in Javanese," ms., University of Texas at Austin.

Uhrbach, A. (1985) "Some Facts of Reduplication in Bahasa Indonesia with Implications for a Theory of Morphology," ms., University of Texas, Austin.

van der Hulst, H. and N. Smith, eds., (1982) *The Structure of Phonological Representations*, Vols. I-II, Foris, Dordrecht.

Weeda. D. (1986) "Madurese Reduplication within Lexical Phonology," ms., University of Texas, Austin.

Wescott, R. W. (1965) Review of Thomas (1963), *Language* 41, 346-7.

Whitney, W. D. (1889) *Sanskrit Grammar*, Thirteenth issue (1973) of the second edition, Harvard University Press, Cambridge, Mass.

Wilbur, R. B. (1973) *The Phonology of Reduplication*, Doctoral dissertation, University of Illinois, Urbana.

Williams, E. (1978) "Across-the-Board Rule Application," _Linguistic Inquiry_ 9, 31-43.

Younes, R. (1983) "The Representation of Geminate Consonants," ms., University of Texas, Austin.

For Product Safety Concerns and Information please contact our EU
representative GPSR@taylorandfrancis.com
Taylor & Francis Verlag GmbH, Kaufingerstraße 24, 80331 München, Germany

www.ingramcontent.com/pod-product-compliance
Lightning Source LLC
Chambersburg PA
CBHW060557230426
43670CB00011B/1864